You are
Inspired

YOU ARE INSPIRED

AN INTUITIVE GUIDE TO LIFE WITH MEANING AND PURPOSE

BY BELINDAGRACE

Author of *You Are Clairvoyant*

ROCKPOOL
PUBLISHING

A Rockpool book
Published by Rockpool Publishing
24 Constitution Road, Dulwich Hill, NSW 2203, Australia
www.rockpoolpublishing.com.au

First published in 2009

National Library of Australia
Cataloguing-in-Publication Entry

BelindaGrace.
You are inspired: an intuitive guide to life with meaning
and purpose / BelindaGrace.

1st ed.

9781921295232 (pbk.)

You are 2.

Self-consciousness (Awareness)
Self.
Success.
Spiritual exercises.
Clairvoyance.

158.1

Edited by Gabiann Marin
Cover and internal design by Liz Seymour, Seymour Designs
Typeset by Value Chain International Ltd, India.
Printed and bound in Australia by Griffin Press

10 9 8 7 6 5 4 3 2 1

CONTENTS

ABOUT THE AUTHOR

BelindaGrace has a thriving practice in Sydney where she deals with private clients from all over the world, and regularly conducts courses and workshops. She is passionate about helping people discover a deeper meaning and purpose to their lives in order to create a sound foundation of emotional and spiritual health, from which all other areas of life can thrive.

In her spare time BelindaGrace loves to enjoy the peace and beauty of her seaside home on Sydney's Northern Beaches.

If you wish to find out more about BelindaGrace and her work please go to www.rockpoolpublishing.com.au, www.belindagrace.com or phone Neutral Bay Health and Wellbeing on 61 2 9953 8503 for an appointment.

INTRODUCTION

I just wanted to say how grateful I am. I have come such a long way within myself in the last six months, I have never felt better and am so excited for my life now and have found so many answers. I really feel that I know myself now and that through being more in touch with my spiritual and emotional levels I can be that strong, beautiful person that I have always wanted to be!

Thank you.

KELLY W.
SYDNEY, AUSTRALIA

Feeling inspired about your life is quite possibly the most important ingredient for happiness and success in all its available forms. That irrepressible urge to leap out of your bed in the morning and get stuck into the day.

It is a matter of great concern to me that so many people do not feel this way. For twelve years now, in my work as a Clairvoyant Healer, I have spoken to thousands of people from Australia and around the world, and from all religions and walks of life. Rich or poor, healthy or ill, attached or single, there is one topic that inevitably comes up, one area where people always seem to seek answers. What is the meaning and purpose of my life, what is it that I am meant to be doing, what is my passion?

One way or another, most people will ask me one of these questions, hoping for some guidance from their Angels or some clues to their confusion in the experiences of their past lives. Usually this topic will arise in the very first consultation and be coupled with an admission that they feel so flat, so unmotivated, so *uninspired*.

The devastating truth is that all of these beautiful people have an incredible combination of gifts, skills and talents that they just don't see.

They may have a job that is unfulfilling or another area of their life that causes them concern, but even when they have 'all the boxes ticked' the lament is still the same. Amazingly I have often noticed that it is the people who are well off financially, in a good relationship, have happy, healthy children and a good career who are *most likely* to feel this way.

'I feel like I am wasting my life' is what so many people confide to me. 'I feel like I should be doing something else, but I don't know what it is.'

Do you hear your own concerns or feelings in any of these conversations?

In these pages you will find simple, easy to use methods to help you approach and dismantle these conundrums. You will be shown how, through developing your own natural intuitive and clairvoyant abilities, you can reconnect to your own, innate sense of inspiration and wonder about the world and your life.

Each of us has the natural ability to feel a sense of joy and purpose; to go through life with the skill of uncovering and creating meaning in a way that makes everyday life something to feel excited about. Through connecting with your inherent intuitive and clairvoyant capacity you too can discover that there is a world of possibility out there for you to explore and enjoy and that, deep down, you really knew how to access it all along.

You will benefit from reading this book because you are now ready to fly. You are ready to let go of your doubt, fear of failure, past disappointments and even cynicism. Your Soul is telling you that these things don't serve you and that there is definitely more to life. Perhaps you feel like you have been walking around in the dark lately. Well, in this book, my Angels, Spirit Guides and I are offering you some Light.

Through these pages you will discover how to tap into your inner wisdom, call profound guidance into your life, lift your own vibrational frequency, set up a balance in your chakras for positive manifestation and more. It's all so simple, all you need to do is show up.

You will see how the majority of people feel, or have felt, the same way and will be given simple suggestions, contemplations and techniques to help you out of that hole you think you have fallen into. Best of all, you will find that life is an amazing adventure and that you are now able to be an adventurer and pioneer.

One of the most inspiring people in my life is my one and only Aunt, who lives in France. Aunty Esther has always loved travel and adventure, whilst her husband, my Uncle Michel, an accomplished professor, loves the cosy home life. She travels here and there with her friends, her work as a librarian and her choir group, whilst Michel stays home whenever he can. One day I asked my Aunt if it bothered her that her husband never travelled anywhere with her, and she said 'Oh, you know, he travels very well in his mind.'

In that moment I understood that his intellect and academic understanding of the world provided a perfect balance to her adventurousness. That he was inspired by books and learning, and she by hands-on experience, and that in their own unique ways they were both explorers; each one just as enthusiastic about the worlds they uncovered on their 'travels'.

And so it is for each of us, to find our own unique ways of exploring and being excited about life. It's about discovering your way and what will make your heart sing, so that when the sun peeks over the horizon each day you leap out of bed to embrace it. It's time to heed the call of your Soul and follow the simple ideas in this book to a life of greater inspiration, meaning and sense of purpose.

CHAPTER ONE

HOW TO GET THE MOST FROM THIS BOOK

BelindaGrace, If I am doing 30 knots in the fog, then you are the Light of Galadriel, shining in the darkness to guide me on my way.

Namasté

MARK B.
SYDNEY, AUSTRALIA

We live in a culture that likes to pretend that you can wave a magic wand and suddenly everything will be just fine. There are 'instant' weight loss products, 'instant' detox products, 'instant' relaxation, rejuvenation, learning, cleaning products … The list goes on and on. Naturally, most of us know that the 'instant' component of the product or service belongs firmly in the realm of marketing and advertising, not in actual reality. Yet still we hope. 'Maybe one application of this bland looking cream will take all my wrinkles away!'

The funny thing about magic wands, however, is that they do exist. They just don't look like we expect them to most of the time and, what's more, when we find one we often say to ourselves, 'No, this isn't going to work for me. Sure it's a magic wand all right, but I will never be able to figure out how to use it.' So, after being handed a magic wand what do we do? We talk ourselves out of using it and accept disappointment and defeat before even starting!

The quote opening this chapter was written to me in an email from a client of mine whom I admire enormously, because he never, ever, ever gave up. Even in the darkest moments of his life, when there seemed very little hope, he just kept going, chipping away at his demons one by one to the best of his ability. Mark's emotional and personal struggles were very similar to many of the clients and students I work with: he had a tendency to sabotage himself every step of the way. Yet no matter how many times he fell over or tripped himself up, he would pick himself up, dust himself off and, determined to have a breakthrough, he would keep working with the guidance that his Angels and Guides had given him. Even the fact that he was backpacking around Asia during some of this time didn't provide an excuse for him. We communicated by email and telephone, conducting readings that way whenever he felt he needed a little more Light.

When I read the email that I have shared with you now, I was so moved I started to cry. It is quite possibly the nicest thing anyone has ever said to me. The transformation in this amazing man's life has been fantastic. Not only has he healed and transformed those aspects of his inner world that used to make his life hell, but the woman he loves has come back into his life and he is on track to develop a career as a talented healer and therapist himself. I know that he will be brilliant at this work because his own healing process will now avail him of an empathy with other people's struggles that you could never glean from mere study alone.

Now he is his own source of Light and will become a source of light for many others in years to come. He is on what Joseph Campbell referred to as 'the Hero's Journey' and it has earned him the right to live fully from his Soul and heart. Every time he dropped one of his magic wands or got frustrated with his supposedly slow progress, he reminded himself that this was the most important journey of his life and that there was no way he wanted to turn back.

If you are like me, you are probably a little bit impatient. So we will get this out of the way right now. This book contains some incredible magic wands; you just have to go ahead and use them. People often ask me about the skills I have as a Clairvoyant Healer – how it is that I can see and communicate with Angels and Spirit Guides so clearly or tap into some past life information with great detail, at will. The simple answer is that I have kept on 'using it'. Once I realised I had some skill in this field I just kept doing a little more every day. The level of ability I have now didn't come to me all at once.

It's the same with the techniques and skills in this book. I have used them over and over again, *even when* I have felt fearful or doubtful; at some point I will get going again, because the alternative of not doing so is not acceptable to me. The *only* difference between me – a person who leaps out of bed at 5 or 6 am eager to get on with my day – and someone who is dreading the day to come is the commitment I have made to living a life I love. Yes, really.

For all you impatient souls out there here is another tip: read the whole book from start to finish first. Then, go back through the book one chapter at a time and complete the exercises suggested in each one. Don't skip any of the exercises, especially if you think you won't like it or don't need to do it. Our monkey minds are great at getting us to skirt around the things that will open the most important of inner doorways.

As you read through each chapter you will find that most of them include a suggested activity, such as writing down your thoughts and feelings on a particular topic or giving yourself a special type of energy balance. Some of the exercises are a one-off or occasional activity, while others will need to be repeated for best effect. When and how often you may best use each technique will be clearly laid out in each chapter.

Why not create a dedicated notebook or journal to use with this book so that you can look back on it later and appreciate your progress.

A note on using your journal – for those of you who already understand and enjoy the great benefits of regular interactions with your journal I don't need to explain why the journalling exercises in this book are so important. For those of you who groan at the idea of having to put pen to paper please take a moment to consider. Writing your own personal thoughts, feelings, ideas and experiences down in a journal that is private and exclusively for you is one of the greatest tools available to us on our path of spiritual growth and self-awareness. The only problem with journalling is that it seems too simple to a lot of people. Many of us have imagined that we have to do something sensational or have some spectacular experiences or events in our lives in order to become 'more spiritual'. Many of us believe that a mind-bending 'ah-ha' moment is necessary in order to gain a high level of awareness or get in touch with our Angels and Spirit Guides and to develop our intuition. Nothing could be further from the truth.

The simple act of writing in your journal is a vital doorway to self discovery, healthy reflection, understanding and awareness. It is cathartic and provides the perfect opportunity for you to express thoughts, feelings, opinions and ideas that are not yet fully formed, too private to share and so on. As you put the words to paper it will help you to have realisations about yourself, strengthen your connection to your Soul and create a space in your life for the expression of a creativity you may as yet be unaware of. Another bonus is that you learn from yourself because as you write about the things you are reflecting on you will see it from a new perspective, which in itself is a form of clarity.

Like meditation, filling a journal with your own words causes you to sit with yourself. It's just you and the words. It causes you to connect with levels of yourself that don't have time to emerge during the course of a busy day. I therefore recommend that you complete the journal exercises in this book as soon as you have read the chapter, or in the morning or evening, before or after the normal activities of your day.

One last thing I should probably mention. Regular journalling can and will lead to channelling information from your Angels, Spirit Guides and other helpful sources. A friend recently told me with great delight that, after years of journalling on a regular basis, she is now receiving direct answers to specific questions when she sits and writes. She knows that she is channelling these answers because the words flow so freely onto her page without any thinking effort on her part. All she has to do is listen and write. So it is not only yourself that you will communicate with in your journal: you will also create a space for your Divine Guidance to come through to communicate with you.

Finally, the best way to get the most out of this book is to use, re-use and keep re-using it, so that the magic can seep in and accumulate. Which brings me to one last point about magic wands. When you are handed one it is not meant to change absolutely everything, completely and utterly, overnight. That would be way too much change for anyone and would dissipate the power of the transformation process itself. It is the time taken during the transformation process that allows us to recognise and assimilate whatever it is we need to learn from our experiences, so that we can be much more aware of similar situations in the future and make more healthy choices the next time around.

The real magic in the magic is that it happens gradually and will transform your life incrementally each time you engage with it. The magic is you. You, uncovering your talents and gifts, your unique ways of expressing yourself, bringing them back to life and sharing them with your world. This is the true meaning of living an inspired and inspiring life.

CHAPTER TWO

How Developing Your Intuition And Clairvoyance Gets You Inspired!

I just want to say thank you for what I am learning, it has been a great inspiration ... I will continue to persevere and practise and gain confidence. You have given me lots of tools and techniques that will help me focus, and, rather than the occasional spontaneous 'readings' I have done in the past, I want to be able to channel it and use it to my full potential. What you have taught me is what I have been looking for, and I know I am guided to do what I need to do when the time is right.

NARELLE P.
SYDNEY, AUSTRALIA

People who live more of their lives by following their intuitive and clairvoyant guidance have a major advantage over those who rely on rationalism and logic. Living intuitively puts you into a space where you are tapping into your most powerful and personal truths. Logical or left-brained living is always subject to change and challenge of an external nature, influenced by the latest findings, fashions, opinions and what is considered acceptable by the status quo. Very rarely does this status quo approach to life have your true best interests at heart.

Conformity ultimately creates a greyness that sits like a pall of mediocrity over the people involved. Because it works to a formula, it can't possibly take into account individual feelings, perceptions and needs, and whilst a certain level of organisation is definitely required to keep the physical aspects of life functioning in a busy, crowded world, it is purely functional. It does not feed the heart or the Soul.

Intuitive, clairvoyant people, however, can function easily, smoothly and successfully in daily life whilst keeping the status quo in a healthy perspective. We understand the need for organisation, but this does not mean that we need to sacrifice our ability to live an inspiring life full of meaning, joy and purpose. The more you live by your intuition and those wonderful feelings of inspiration, a stronger sense of inner knowing will emerge. This will lead you to trust yourself more; which is one of the most satisfying feelings a person can have.

When you start to live your life from a place of self-awareness and self-trust you allow the previously dominant style of thinking – the monkey mind, as my Angels and Guides often refer to it – to fall away. Your monkey or ego-based mind is the voice in your head that is always comparing yourself to others, saying you aren't good enough, questioning your feelings and telling you that you have to get it right all the time. It is the part of your consciousness that really believes you would be happier if only you had a new car, a bigger house or could just lose those last two kilos. In short, your monkey mind is never secure, content or satisfied and our whole consumer-based lifestyle is designed to manipulate it.

The thinking or 'monkey' mind can only operate from the limited standpoint of what is considered factual and/or acceptable to others. We only have to look around us to see the effects that living from the monkey mind has had on our lives and our world.

Following your inner guidance equals fulfilment and success because you become the one who decides what is fulfilling and successful for you in your own life. The importance of being able to accept yourself in this way cannot be overstated. When you finally let go enough to follow what feels right for you, rather than do what you think might be the best thing, or what you think is expected of you, life automatically becomes easier and more enjoyable.

The thing that everyone is looking for, the thing that so many people feel is missing from their lives, is not another possession, nor is it another hobby, partner, child, dress size or job. The amazing clients and students who come to me with these big questions about life already, intuitively, know this, which is why the big questions are pressing them forward. The thing that is missing from our lives is our connection to our true, authentic, uncomplicated inner selves. As you increasingly connect to your intuitive and clairvoyant guidance, you are rebuilding a connection to the inspired Being that you are at your essence. Your deep inner knowing and wisdom, combined with your innate ability to tap into wisdom beyond your personal ability to know, will guide you to the centre of yourself and when you connect with that inner truth a growing awareness of how to live an inspired life is inevitable.

Interestingly, this may well lead you to go and buy another possession, take up a new hobby, leave or find a partner, have another child and so on. The big difference will be in the 'why', in the meaning behind your choices and actions and the sense of purpose you feel in making and doing them, but for life to be truly meaningful and fulfilling a clear sense of 'why' needs to come first, otherwise it will just be another addition to a string of meaningless possessions or actions. So, a stronger connection to your intuitive and clairvoyant guidance – what I call my 'Little

Voice' – is the key to the 'why' of life, that ineffable feeling of excitement and inspiration that makes life worthwhile.

A LITTLE EXPERIENCE OF MY OWN

I have been a vegetarian for almost 20 years. People have often asked me why I chose to be a vegetarian as they felt it was something that would be difficult or even boring to maintain.

I had all the usual reasons for my preferred diet. I felt better when I didn't eat meat; my digestion functioned more easily and so on. But sometimes, if I felt the person I was speaking with was really interested, I would tell them about an experience I had after one of the spiritual development classes I used to attend before I became a Clairvoyant Healer.

During a meditation my teacher told us that she would help us open up to the emotions of animals, including the suffering they endure at the hands of human beings. I wasn't very switched on in those days, or so I believed, so I just sat there enjoying the meditation but not feeling a great deal.

Arriving home after class that evening I was hungry and opened the cupboard to scout around for some ingredients for dinner. The first thing I saw was a can of tuna with a picture of a dolphin on it and the words 'Dolphin Safe' on the front. I looked at this tin and simply burst into tears. In that moment I felt very deeply the impact that my diet was having on the animals and the natural world around me. I had been a vegetarian on and off for some years before, but now I had a whole new 'why' and felt completely inspired to commit to that way of life.

This new sense of commitment then led me to amazing books such as Diet for a Small Planet *by Frances Moore Lappé and* The Last Hours of Ancient Sunlight *by Thom Hartmann. These books in turn inspired me to take a further interest in the real impact that we human beings have on our Earth and how a big picture view of our daily actions is vital to the survival of all who inhabit her.*

Everyone's 'why' is unique and personal. The time has come to begin reconnecting with yours.

CHAPTER THREE

CHAKRA AND CHANNEL ACTIVATION

People are like stained-glass windows. They sparkle and shine when the sun is out, but when the darkness sets in their true beauty is revealed only if there is a light from within.

ELIZABETH KUBLER ROSS
AUTHOR AND PSYCHIATRIST
1926–2004

When it comes to getting the basics right, this chakra and channel activation exercise is fantastic. Shown to me in a moment of inspiration on the beach one morning, it is a delightful and simple breath and movement exercise to help you start your day or to give yourself a refreshing energy pick-me-up any time you like.

We call it the 'Thanksgiving to Mother Earth', but it is so much more than that, and although this lovely exercise activates your channel and the seven main chakras, clears your energy field and surrounds you in a high-vibrational energy and Light, it only takes between thirty and sixty seconds to complete. Perfect!

In order to develop your natural intuitive and clairvoyant abilities it is important to keep the most important areas of your spiritual anatomy clear, healthy and strong. I never stop using the simple methods I have learned over the years, including this one, because the channel and chakras need ongoing maintenance, just like our physical anatomy does. In fact the condition of your spiritual anatomy can never be too good, there is always room for improvement, which in turn will strengthen your connection to your Divine Guidance and help to keep you on your intuitive and clairvoyant path. The final step is also an act of surrounding yourself with positive energy and Light – what some people like to think of as protection. So as you can see it is a wonderful way to set yourself up for the day.

Last but not least, this simple exercise is a way of offering your thanks, support and blessing to our beautiful planet and gives you a moment to connect with Her and to acknowledge that *everything* we eat, drink and use on a daily basis comes from the endless and forgiving bounty of Nature. Mother Earth is a Soul and Being in Her own right and connecting deliberately with Her will always help you to enhance your sense of awareness and belonging.

THANKSGIVING TO MOTHER EARTH

REQUIREMENTS: A place where you can stand comfortably with plenty of room to move your arms outwards in a circular motion and enough room to bend forward. My favourite place is the beach.

OPTIONAL: You can stand facing in any direction you choose, but if a particular direction feels significant to you, such as East in the morning for sunrise, then you are free to face that way if you like.

TIME REQUIRED: 30 to 60 seconds.

HOW OFTEN SHOULD I DO IT? Once a day.

◆ Start by standing in a relaxed manner with your arms by your side. If you wish to face in a particular direction, such as East for the sunrise, West for the sunset or in the direction of a place or compass point that holds a special meaning for you, then orientate yourself to that direction before you begin.

◆ Breathe deeply and relax, contemplating your intention to connect to Mother Earth, activate and refresh your channel and chakras and surround yourself in an uplifting and nurturing energy and Light.

◆ Bring your hands together in front of your heart chakra as in prayer position.

◆ Breathe out and then, on a long, slow in-breath, circle your hands upwards and outwards making two big symmetrical circles in front of you with each hand. Make the circle upwards and outwards until your hands circle back down and in to the centre, touching in front of your heart chakras again. Make three complete circles on the one, long in-breath.

◆ By now your lungs should be feeling very full, your chest nicely expanded and your hands pressed together in front of you after completing the third circle.

◆ Then, as you exhale fully, bend down slowly and touch the ground. You may keep your legs straight or bend your knees, whichever is more comfortable for you.

◆ Make sure that you expel all the air in your lungs. Keep exhaling while your hands are on the ground and say out loud or in your mind "Thank You, Mother Earth" and imagine that as you exhale all your breath and touch the ground or floor you are sending energy and love into our planet. Imagine yourself wrapping your arms around Her in a loving embrace.

Note: during the exhale, whilst placing my palms on the ground and sending all my energy, love and gratitude into the Earth, I like to imagine myself hugging our planet as a way of saying thank you for all the natural beauty She provides. I like to think of some of the wonderful places I have been or hope to visit one day, or even to picture a region that might need a little bit of extra nurturing, such as a wartorn or drought-stricken place in the world. Use the exhalation as an opportunity to linger and contemplate for a few moments.

◆ This part of the process is a relaxation and letting go for you as well. In the first step you inhale oxygen, along with prana or chi to energise yourself, so the exhalation is also an opportunity to cleanse and clear. Let your upper body hang loosely from your waist or hips as you bend forward, allow your arms to be soft and to dangle. Bend your knees as much as you need to so you can at least get your fingertips to, or close to, the ground.

◆ Once you have emptied your lungs and uttered your blessing, touch the tops of your feet with your fingertips and start to inhale very slowly and rise gradually, while keeping your back soft and curled over. Running your fingertips up the surface of your feet, ankles and legs, imagine yourself drawing rich red energy and Light up from the core of Mother Earth, up into your feet and legs.

◆ Continue to fill your lungs with air while sliding your hands up the surface of your legs to your hips. Then put one hand to the front of your base chakra and one hand to the back at the base of your spine, bringing the red light into your hips and base chakra.

◆ This last step could take a little practice, because you have seven chakras to touch and draw Light into, all on the one, long in-breath. So make sure you breathe in very slowly. Imagine the air you are breathing in to be like a long slender ribbon. Don't gasp, you will fill up your lungs soon enough.

◆ Keeping one hand palm down onto the front of your body and one hand with the palm facing onto the back of your body, continue to breathe in, and as you now bring your hands up to your navel chakra you can picture orange light flowing into it as well.

◆ Moving both hands upwards in a graceful, continuous motion, bring them up to your solar plexus chakra just above your belly button and feel it being infused with yellow light. Then to the heart chakra letting it be filled with green light.

Note: most people are able to touch the fronts and backs of their chakras with either the palm or the back of their hands. The heart chakra can be a bit tricky though, unless you are quite flexible through your shoulders. If you find the back of your heart chakra difficult to reach, don't strain yourself, just get your finger tips as close as you can or bring both hands to the front of your body for that chakra. This is not a gymnastics workout: your intention is the most important thing, so just

*do the best you can. If you do bring both hands to the front
for the heart chakra remember to take one hand behind your
neck again for the throat chakra.*

◆ Continue moving your hands upwards, one to the back
of your neck and one to the front of your throat chakra,
letting it be filled with beautiful, blue light and then up
to the brow with the indigo coloured light. Finally you
will bring both hands to the top of your head to fill your
crown chakra with violet light.

*Note: After practising this a few times you will find it easy to
move your hands continuously from one chakra to the next,
visualising each new colour coming in as you go. It is lovely
to pause for a second or two on each chakra and to name
the colour of each one as you come to it. So as you come to
place your hands on your base chakra you can say to yourself
or out loud "red", then on to the navel chakra say "orange",
the solar plexus chakra say "yellow" and so on.*

◆ While both hands are still resting on the top of your
head, take one more breath of air into your lungs. Really
fill them to capacity!

◆ Then, with a strong and controlled exhalation, expel all
your air whilst gracefully lowering your arms around you
and then bringing them up and lowering them all around
you again several times while you breathe out. Perhaps
you will feel like a ballet dancer taking many bows!

◆ As you move your arms about you in this manner say to

yourself, "I now surround myself in gold and white light" and picture your whole energy field being filled with this magnificent energy.

- Once you have exhaled fully and have put the gold and white light all around you take a moment to stand still with your arms resting by your side.

- Well done! You have now completed the 'Thanksgiving to Mother Earth' and activated your channel and chakras and surrounded yourself in a lovely energy and Light in the process.

I actually enjoy doing this exercise so much that I will often complete four rounds of it, one after the other, facing towards a different point of the compass each time. I like to honour all the elements of Nature in this way – Earth, Wind, Fire and Water. At the very least I thoroughly recommend that you complete this exercise once a day. There is no best time really, but the morning always seems ideal to me because of the way it wakes up the spiritual anatomy, starts the day with an expression of gratitude, gets air into the lungs and sends a positive vibration throughout the energy field. For those of you who like the idea of protection, particularly if you have to go into a stressful or negative working environment, this is an especially healthy way to begin your day.

You can use the 'Thanksgiving to Mother Earth' any time

and as many times as you like throughout the day also. So if you forget to perform it in the morning go and find a private spot wherever you are and do it there, or use it for a special lift before a demanding meeting, going to visit someone in hospital or any other potentially stressful situation you know you are going to deal with during your day.

Follow the above instructions to the best of your ability, but remember, you can't really get it wrong, it's your intention that counts. So give it your best shot and you will still get all the benefit. The Angels gave this to us to help us feel better, not to put us to the test. Enjoy!

IAN'S EXPERIENCE

Ian is a very successful businessman who has come to understand the importance of inspiration and intuition in all aspects of his life.

One of the most frustrating occurrences in life is blocked piping. There is only a trickle getting through and it takes a specialist to rectify the problem. Our intuition relies on us being able to get clear messages. When our channel and chakras are blocked, only a trickle of information gets through. BelindaGrace is a specialist in assisting people to unblock their channel and chakras and shows you how to keep them healthy.

Since learning this technique my flow of intuition has increased to a gushing pipe, which has helped me in my personal and business life.

IAN RALSTON
COMPANY DIRECTOR

CHAPTER FOUR

WHAT IS INSPIRATION?

I used to think that feeling inspired about life was something that only happened for other people. I never imagined I could feel truly enthusiastic about my life. I always just plodded along, getting by and living from one day to the next. I had very little sense of the bigger picture, but something in me was determined to figure it out and to find a way to become inspired.

BRETT McT.
BRISBANE, AUSTRALIA

Inspiration is a very powerful feeling that is unmistakable when it comes. I believe that everyone is born with the ability to feel inspired, but that all manner of circumstances and experiences in life can lead us to mistrust and repress that feeling, let alone act on it. The process of reconnecting with your own inspired nature is not what our consumer-based society portrays it to be. We are taught to believe that we have to find the person, place or thing first and then we will feel inspired. But, as you can easily see all around you, the monkey mind quickly becomes bored and dissatisfied with the new person, place or thing.

Worse still, you may even wind up blaming those external factors in your life for deceiving you or letting you down, prompting you to feel disillusioned about life, believing that if only you could find that elusive possession, activity or individual, then everything would be great and your life would be filled with meaning and purpose overnight.

Our cupboards full of stuff that we are no longer interested in and the ever increasing divorce rates world wide make it clear that looking for inspiration outside of ourselves is not the solution.

Even when you feel genuinely inspired by the actions and triumphs of others, your euphoria is usually short lived and subject to any information or experience that may later contradict that feeling. So how, then, do you begin to uncover that ability to inspire yourself and to feel inspired about your own life on a daily basis?

Reconnecting with your natural ability to feel inspired, and to inspire others in your turn, is a process of learning to trust your feelings and intuition once more. As you start to exercise those intuitive muscles you become more accustomed to that 'Little Voice' inside you that gives you the clues, hints and clear directions towards the kind of life that you desire. It's all about developing a level of spiritual maturity that enables you to understand that your ability to feel inspired comes from within.

Feeling inspired is about reconnecting with that sense of enthusiasm and excitement that may well have been missing from your life for some time. Isn't it interesting, and even strange, that as adults we love to see children laughing, playing and exploring. We totally accept and are often uplifted by their natural enthusiasm and curiosity as we observe how they live life with gusto, clearly expressing their pleasure and displeasure as they feel it.

Yet as adults we are so much more self conscious. The need to appear cool, knowing, in control, on top of things, smarter than others or whatever you would like to call it are some of the things that get in the way of feeling inspired. Acting as though you already know what is going on or going to happen is the natural enemy of spontaneity – another essential ingredient in an inspired and meaningful life. They are also the natural enemies of living through your intuitive and clairvoyant abilities. So, part of the process of getting back in touch with your inner source of inspiration is your willingness to let go of the need to have all the answers, and to live more in the present moment.

Your version of inspiration and what you find inspiring is unique to you. Although this may seem obvious, it is a very important truth to remember. Constantly comparing yourself to others and doing what you believe you need to do in order to 'fit in' are more sure-fire ways to kill off inspiration. There are some programs on television that I find particularly fascinating in this regard. Be it digging up old archaeological ruins, discussing the origin and value of antiques or interviewing a collector about his or her amazing collection of unusual stamps, clocks, tractors or china dolls, what strikes me again and again is how passionate these people are about what they do, how much joy it brings into their lives and how they continually 'dare to be different' in the pursuit of what they love.

If you allow it to, your natural intuitive and clairvoyant nature will guide you towards the things you love as well.

To some extent, conformity is actually a survival mechanism. The law of the jungle makes it pretty clear that if you stand out from the herd too much you could either be challenged or be attacked. Despite the fact that we human beings consider ourselves to be so advanced, evolved and sophisticated compared to animals, we live a surprisingly large proportion of our lives as though we are still in that jungle.

Heaven forbid that you should draw attention to yourself

by collecting a certain type of item that nobody else seems interested in, partaking in an activity that is outside the mould you were supposedly created in, or even just getting excited about something from time to time. Virtually the only time anyone is allowed to cheer and jump for joy these days is when their team wins the grand final! The rest of the time we go out of our way to appear logical, practical and rational.

WHAT INSPIRES YOU NOW?

REQUIREMENTS: A notebook or journal and a pen.

OPTIONAL: A quiet, pleasant place to sit, away from all the usual distractions. Some uplifting music to create a lovely atmosphere.

TIME REQUIRED: A minimum of ten minutes or as long as you like.

HOW OFTEN SHOULD I DO IT? At least once, after that you can add to your lists any time you like.

- **Part One** – Write a list of anything that inspires you now or has inspired you in the past. You may wish to create a page for each topic, such as 'People who inspire me now', 'People who inspired me in the past', 'People who I have never met who inspire me', 'Organisations/groups/causes that inspire me', 'Ideas and concepts that inspire me', 'Activities that inspire me', 'Music that inspires me', 'Places that inspire me', 'Books that inspire/have inspired me', 'Movies that inspire/have inspired me' and so on. Create as many categories as you like or just get it all out onto the page as it comes, in no particular order.

- If your tendency is to sit there and say to yourself "oh, I can't think of *anything*" you will need to persevere! That is why the required time for this exercise is a minimum of ten minutes. You need to allow time for your memories to percolate up from the depths of your subconscious mind.

- Notice the feelings of excitement that start to well up from within you as those memories of people, places and things that inspire you dawn on you once more.

- Do not repress the urge to laugh out loud, cry or dance around the room!

- Keep scribbling away furiously until you have ferreted out every source of inspiration you can think of. Do not critique any of your responses. If the bold girl with the bright red hair and freckles, back in sixth grade, inspired you because she spoke up to a teacher who was being unfair, then so be it! Nobody else has to see what you have written down. It's up to you whether you choose to share it or not.

- **Part Two** – On a new page write the heading 'Things I would like to feel inspired about from now on'. Then write down whatever it is you feel you genuinely want to get inspired about. For example, you may wish to become more inspired about your fitness and health, being more active in your community, taking up a certain hobby or learning a new skill.

- Carry your journal around with you in your handbag or brief case; or keep it in a handy place at home so you can add to any of your lists whenever a new form of inspiration springs to mind.

- Read over your lists to see if you can notice any themes or trends. Are there certain types of people, activities, places or interests that consistently appear?

- Make a note of all and any ideas that spring to mind that will help you bring these inspiring things into your life as an ongoing or regular experience.

Note: did you know that feeling inspired, excited and enthusiastic about the things in your life – past or present – is synonymous with gratitude? When you connect with those lovely, positive feelings towards something or someone you immediately generate a feeling of thanks towards them and your energy says "I am so grateful for the part you have played in my life!". Gratitude is a magical energy which can bring so much more good your way. Feelings of inspiration feed into feelings of gratitude and vice versa, allowing you to connect with that inspired and grateful core of yourself and bringing you double the benefits.

My hope is that you will find this exercise truly enjoyable. It will help you to remember all that has been good about your life. I do recommend that you re-read your lists several times over the next few days to help bring any themes or trends into focus, just in case they weren't obvious on the day you first wrote them.

A couple of years ago a client of mine did a version of this exercise and noticed that his list of movies that inspired him was enormous. He also noticed that many of the people who had inspired him over the years were creative and artistic types. At this point in time he worked in I.T. doing long hours in the office without much thought of or time for hobbies. He was a fairly athletic fellow, so he made time for sport and fitness, but had that nagging feeling that something was missing from his life.

After going over his lists he realised that he loved cinema and the way that a good movie could make people think, bring new ideas and even controversial topics to a wide audience, and of course entertain and uplift. He didn't throw away his job and run off to Hollywood, he just joined a local amateur group that made short films, joined a movie club and invited his friends to any event where new and interesting movies were being screened. Most of his life remained the same in terms of what he was doing, but he found an enormous amount of fulfilment and satisfaction by making time in his life for a passion he had not fully realised he had. This in turn brought him into contact with new people of similar interests, and so it goes on. You never know where a few small steps in a new direction might lead you.

A recent discovery of my own was when it dawned on me that I love watching one of the weekly gardening programs on television. I had never thought of myself as a gardener, amazed that my few pot pants had managed to survive my sporadic attentions. Then one Sunday morning about four months ago I woke up with the idea that I was going to go to my local garden centre and buy some plants, compost and whatever else they advised. Following this strong urge without question, I took measurements and photographs of the area I wanted to plant and off I went. I had a vague idea that I would like to grow some vegetables, but had no idea what was possible.

After chatting with the staff there – and thoroughly enjoying the whole learning process – I came away with a car boot full of plants and materials. Since then I have learned how to plant and grow quite a few things with success. It has been such a thrill! I eat my own rocket and lettuce, take my home-grown cherry tomatoes to friends when I visit and have two gorgeous bougainvilleas working their way up the back fence. I get very excited talking to other gardeners now and picking their brains for handy hints and information. I have literally stepped into a whole new world. My intuition told me that the time was right for me to get started; what a shame it would have been if I had talked myself out of it and let myself be defeated before giving it a try.

KERRYN'S EXPERIENCE

When Kerryn came along to my five-day intensive course she soon sensed that most of the other students were progressing more quickly than her. She was amazed at how readily they seemed to take to the work, seeing colours in the chakras, getting some visual information about past lives and being able to describe the appearance of the Angels and Spirit Guides who came to them. In actual fact, none of the other students were mastering all the techniques first up, but that was how Kerryn perceived it.

I was able to get a clear sense of energy moving and flowing and lots of feelings. I'm an empathetic, emotional sort of person, and feelings seemed to be the way Spirit chose to communicate with me and I felt really inspired by what we were learning, but I just wished I could see something with my clairvoyant sight like the other students were.

As the course continued I started to receive stronger and clearer messages and information in verbal form, but still no pictures. Occasionally, BelindaGrace would check in to make sure I wasn't feeling left out, but my gut feel – another way of describing intuition – was that I was in the right place. There was no way that I was going to let any doubt seep in, although I did jokingly refer to myself as the 'runt of the litter'!

Despite the fact that my clairvoyant sight had not opened up during the five days of the course, I never allowed my disappointment at not 'seeing' to distract the other students and in the end I graduated with flying colours and returned home to rural New South Wales.

I decided not to let my lack of 'clairvoyance' stop me using the lessons I had learned, so I rented a room at the local natural therapies centre and did chakra balances and readings for friends, fellow practitioners and even a few paying customers. Within two weeks I began having my first experiences of clairvoyant sight and could describe scenes from past lives and descriptions of Angels to my clients. Suddenly, I was absolutely delighted with my progress.

KERRYN
NSW, AUSTRALIA

During her first month Kerryn didn't make any money, but the confidence and experience she gained were priceless. She knew that she was on the right path and her confidence and skills have continued to grow.

Today she is working at the same natural therapies centre two days a week, seeing up to five paying clients a day. Kerryn is so pleased that she listened to her inner guidance and didn't give up. Not only has she established herself as a Clairvoyant Healer in her local area but she is also going to train with me to become a facilitator of my one-day workshops. When I suggested to Kerryn that I run a workshop in her town she immediately set about organising a venue, catering and publicity, creating a fantastically successful day attended by thirty people from all over that part of the countryside. It was her passion and enthusiasm that motivated me to offer her the traineeship for the one-day workshops because I enjoy being around someone who inspires me.

And so it is when you follow your intuition and gut-feel, when you find that inspiration inside of you to help you keep going, rather than losing heart. You never now where it might lead and you can never be truly sure of what is possible until you get there.

CHAPTER FIVE

BECOMING INSPIRED

When I was a child growing up in the green countryside of Europe my childhood fantasy was to meet a cowboy and ride off into the sunset in the wild west, just like we saw in the Hollywood movies of the day. I always thought it was just a silly day dream, a young girl's fancy, but when I came to Australia and saw that rugged, brown countryside, the cattle and the whole lifestyle, I knew I was in the right place.

It took many years for me to get my farm, but I eventually got there. Now I have cattle and horses of my own and mix with people who have grown up working on the land. I found my cowboy too! It is a dream come true.

INGRID G.
OUTBACK AUSTRALIA

All of us have dreams that we would like to fulfil in this lifetime. Some of those dreams are things that you conceived of as an adult, but many of them would have their foundations in what you dreamed of doing, being and having when you were young. We all had childhood dreams that have been put to one side, so now it is time to give yourself permission to properly contemplate those dreams and consider how they could be brought into reality in your adult life.

Your first reaction may be that most of your childhood dreams were more like fantasies. Nothing particularly practical or useful for your life now. Which is why you need to slow down and take the time to contemplate and go over them. As a child it is most likely that your imagination would have been much more free and active. The imagination uses metaphor and analogy to express itself, so a simple example might be that you 'fantasised' about being a prima ballerina, scooting across a stage in a beautiful tutu. In reality, what you may have found was that ballet lessons are hard work and it takes years of commitment and dedication to become a professional ballerina. You may have naturally given the interest up because of those factors, but the love of ballet and all its inherent beauty will most likely still be with you. Take a moment to think about what ballet and ballerinas represent to you. Is it their gracefulness, femininity, the poetry of their movements, their elusiveness, the lovely music they dance to, or the fact that they can be at the centre of everyone's attention for a while?

Whatever feelings and longings the idea of being a ballerina stirred in you will provide clues to ways you can develop a sense of meaning in your life now. Having a strong desire to create more beauty in the world is a wonderful thing and might be just the kind of inspiration you are looking for. Maybe you work in a very left-brained, chrome and glass type of environment. Ballet can also represent romance, not just in the sense of an actual relationship, but in the more general sense of a life infused with romance and love. This may prompt you to put a vase of peonies on your desk, wear floral prints to work instead of navy or black, or take up an exercise class with an emphasis on music and movement. If you have a romantic, elegant and feminine side to your nature that hasn't seen the light of day much lately, you will definitely enjoy giving it greater expression.

Next time someone tells you that they have no idea what to buy you for your next birthday or the coming Christmas, why not ask them for a ticket to a ballet performance near you? Join a couple of dance company mailing lists or book a ticket to a ballet in a city you are visiting on your next business trip or holiday. You have nothing to lose and may find that you can reconnect with a beautiful childhood dream, returning a source of inspiration to your life without having to go to the trouble of being a ballerina yourself.

For men you might immediately think of the childhood dream of becoming a fireman, train driver or policeman. In a more profound sense, a longing such as this can often show a quality in the man's character that is community service orientated, with a desire to do real good and help others.

A friend of mine is a crew leader and officer with the Rural Fire Service. Anyone who has grown up or lived in Australia knows how fierce our summer bushfire season can be. So it is no small thing to offer yourself to this kind of work. It requires rigorous training during your leisure time on weekends; considerable reading and awareness of safety measures, a willingness to work in a team, follow instructions well and also to lead others. In short, it requires discipline and commitment.

On chatting to my friend about this recently he also told me of the many rewards he receives by being involved. He has made friends with other volunteers, learned many skills and discovered many things about what he is capable of. It means a lot to him to make a positive contribution to his community and he feels inspired by taking part in something bigger than himself. It was very interesting to me to discover that a demonstration from the men of the local fire station was what caught his imagination and made an indelible impression on him when he was at school, at the ripe old age of twelve.

During the demonstration the fireman asked for a volunteer he could work with to act out a rescue from a burning building. My friend put his hand up and was chosen. While taking part in that demonstration he had a powerful feeling that this was a very important and worthwhile thing to do. The feeling stuck with him and has served as his motivation to be involved with volunteer fire services throughout his life.

The things that you dreamed of or that made a strong impression on you when you were young, open hearted and less prone to living life in your head, can provide important clues to what will inspire you as an adult. As you can see by the above examples, you don't need to translate the vision literally into your adult life or try to turn it into a full-time career. There are so many ways that you can make it work for you.

A simple example from my own life relates to the absolute fascination I had for Egyptian art, history, religion and culture from very early on in my childhood. I would literally get goosebumps when there was a television show about the pyramids and loved to pore over books about mummies, hieroglyphics and so on. So Egypt was definitely on my list as a 'must see' travel destination. I went there when I was 23 and, of course, it was amazing. The urge to go there had been so strong all my life and I just soaked the whole experience up like a sponge. Little did I realise at the time I had actually had a past life as an architect in Egypt way back when. So I was also reconnecting with something on a personal, karmic level. Travelling through Egypt was a wonderful realisation of a childhood dream and was certainly an inspiring experience.

That's another thing about fulfilling childhood ideals; it brings you a sense of accomplishment and satisfaction. I may not get to all the places in the world that I would like to explore in this lifetime, but I have been to the ones that were most alluring to me and even if I never get to those places again I have the photos and the beautiful memories to carry with me forever. I have no doubt that if I had not yet been to Egypt and kept putting it off for practical reasons I would be feeling incomplete and be harbouring a deep sense of restlessness about it.

When you were a child your natural intuitive and clairvoyant abilities were much more active. You had not yet learned the ordinary ways of operating in this world. Your imagination was not just something you used to make up stories; it was something you used to express those things about yourself that could be difficult to explain in a rational way. It is also one of the ways that your Soul and intuition communicates with your conscious mind. Words can be very clumsy and are easily misinterpreted; when you are young you don't have a large vocabulary, so the language of intuition, imagination and Soul is often communicated in pictures (dreams and day dreams), feelings and inexplicable longings.

Perhaps you have also yearned to go to certain countries, or do certain things that have nothing to do with your nationality, family background or immediate environment. Your intuition was doing its best to show you a pathway that would be meaningful for you in some way, and if you haven't explored many of them yet it is time to start doing so now.

Whatever it is that will have you leaping out of bed in the morning with excitement and verve will have a unique and personal hue. It is not meant to impress anyone else. Yet something magical happens when you start to explore your passions in life; you begin to attract people and circumstances to you that are compatible with your interests and needs. Soon, rather than thinking that you are a bit of an oddball because none of your existing friends like using oracle cards, attending astrology seminars, walking dogs at the local animal shelter or making enormous patchwork quilts, you will find that some of your friends will admit to having had a similar interest all their lives and they'll join you, or you will meet new people and make new friends.

LETTING YOUR CHILDHOOD DREAMS INSPIRE YOU

REQUIREMENTS: Your journal and a pen.
Somewhere quiet and comfortable to sit down and write.

OPTIONAL: Take a trip down memory lane before
you start writing. Pull out and gather around you
any old photo albums, scrap books, craft items or
beloved possessions you have hung on to for years.
Anything that will help you to remember what you loved
as a child.

TIME REQUIRED: A minimum of 30 minutes.
Give yourself time to contemplate, remember and write.

HOW OFTEN SHOULD I DO IT? At least once, and then any
time you would like to explore further.

◆ Take as long as you need to go through any memorabilia
you may have gathered together. Allow the memories
associated with them to surface and note them down
in your journal. If you have trouble remembering your
childhood you may even benefit by contacting relatives
and friends who knew you then and could relate their

memories to you. It can often be quite amazing to get this kind of feedback.

An old friend might say to you "Gee, you were always so good at XYZ, we all wished we could be more like you!" or "Yes, I remember, whenever there was a stray cat or dog, or an injured bird on the ground, you were there right away patting, feeding and caring for it. I always thought of you as someone who really loved animals." It is incredible what we can forget about ourselves in the headlong rush to grow up and survive.

Make sure you write down anything and everything that comes to you, no matter how trivial or childish it seems. You can add to your list of recollections any time you like and should re-read your list from time to time. Ask yourself, "What was it that I so enjoyed about playing with that particular doll, making tea and cake for everyone, or pretending that I lived underwater amongst the fish and coral?" Let your intuition guide you to the threads that connect your passions in childhood to the things that still interest you today and let your memories unfold so that they can illustrate to you other dreams and fascinations that you may have long forgotten.

♦ Take action – within a week of rediscovering one thing that you were excited about and loved doing as a child, create a way to bring that feeling and experience back into your adult life. If you always wanted to be a pilot go to the local airstrip and take a scenic flight. If you always wanted to be a mountaineer go and grab a book about Sir Edmund Hillary or Lincoln Hall. If you always wanted to be a photographer go and sign up for a photography course at your local community college. If you always wanted to help others and make a difference in the world then go talk to your local charities and volunteer some of your time.

Whether you are old or young, fit or infirm, rich or just making ends meet, there is *always* something you can do to bring your childhood dreams back to life and create a greater sense of meaning and purpose every day.

Another wonderful bonus is that it gives your working life more meaning as well. How so? You may ask. Well, look at it this way; if you can't turn your newly revived passion or interest into a career or a business then your existing work becomes a means to that fulfilling end. No longer do you go to work just to pay the mortgage and the bills. You work because it allows you to afford those trips to Egypt and Machu Picchu, because you need money to pay for all those oil paints and canvases, or to buy the best seats at the opera or ballet. Maybe we would all like to have enough money to pursue our dream activities all day long, but if you don't, then having enough money to enjoy them on the weekend and make the most of your vacation time is the next best thing. Be grateful for the time and money you have and use it doing things that thrill your Soul, and soon enough you will feel much more grateful for whatever income you have.

Not having enough time is an excuse that just isn't going to wash any more either. If finding meaning, purpose, passion and fulfilment really means that much to you then you need to make the time. When you feel genuinely inspired about your life you automatically have more energy, more get-up-and-go. Minor concerns and worries melt away, niggling aches and pains disappear, and the world becomes fresh and fascinating all over again. Switch the television off and take yourself back out there into the world.

Peter's Experience

A few months ago during one of his readings, I was asked by one of his Angels to encourage Peter to do the Let childhood dreams inspire you, exercise.

I found this exercise very difficult because I had been put into a home when I was three years old and was moved around between a few foster families before settling in Perth at the age of thirteen. I had never been able to accumulate much from my childhood and many of my memories were painful ones with strong feelings of being unwanted and not knowing where I truly belonged.

Fortunately the family I settled with were very kind and loving and my life became much more enjoyable from the age of thirteen onwards. One thing I did bring with me to my new home in Western Australia was a collection of watches – some working, some not and some very old and dilapidated.

When I grew up I went into my father's air conditioning business and forgot all about this childhood fascination. It wasn't until I completed this exercise nearly thirty years later that the memories of this fascination with watches and my love of cleaning and repairing them came back to me.

When I rang my mother to ask her what she remembered about me when I first came to live with them, she spoke about the toiletry bag full of watches and watch parts I had brought along. This recollection of hers triggered a flood of memories of my own. Tears even came to my eyes, and I remembered how much I had loved all those watches.

I think when I was very young the watches, no matter how old or broken they were, seemed like a kind of treasure to me. Something that I could keep for myself. We didn't have much space or privacy in the children's home and when I was moved I had to travel light and take only my basic needs with me. I seemed to have a knack for finding discarded watches and enjoyed the challenge of puzzling them back together.

A few days after doing this exercise I found myself on the internet searching out clubs, collectors groups and restoration books and classes. It took a while, but soon I made some interesting discoveries and contacts. From there it grew into a wonderful interest and hobby. I learned, and am still learning, how to restore antique watches and clocks; I trade them on the internet and have a small collection of interesting pieces. I am even saving for a trip to Europe to go to some of the famous watch and clock museums over there.

I don't think I would ever have revived my love of watches in such a way without going through with that exercise, talking to my Mum and writing my thoughts down in that journal. It has certainly made a big difference to my life

PETER
SYDNEY, AUSTRALIA

CHAPTER SIX

BEFRIENDING YOUR INTUITIVE MIND

The most beautiful thing we can experience is the mysterious. It is the source of all true art and all science. Those to whom this emotion is a stranger, who can no longer pause to wonder and stand rapt in awe, are as good as dead: their eyes are closed.

ALBERT EINSTEIN
THEORETICAL PHYSICIST
1879–1955

Your clairvoyant or intuitive mind knows a lot more about life, the Universe and everything than you realise. It is virtually impossible to explain it in physical terms, because there is no plug or socket that we can see with our naked eyes, but whatever 'mind' is, beyond the conscious one we are aware of, it has a direct line to an unlimited wisdom. The famous psychologist Carl Jung referred to this as the collective consciousness; great intuitives such as Edgar Cayce knew it as the Akashic Records. Whatever 'It' is, there is definitely a whole other level of higher awareness and understanding of which we can avail ourselves.

What we tend to think of as our intuition or subconscious mind interacts with this wealth of guidance and information constantly. Simple examples abound, such as knowing who is calling you before you pick the phone up, feeling a strong urge to contact someone only to find out they have recently been thinking about you, or are having problems and need your help. Only a few weeks ago my intuitive mind woke me at 2am to let me know that I had filled out a form incorrectly three days prior. It was an authority for a certain organisation to make direct debits from my bank account, but the way I had filled it in meant that they would have drawn down double the amount they were supposed to. Both myself and the manager at the branch double checked this paper work at the time yet neither of us noticed this mistake. My intuitive mind worked it all out without any conscious effort on my part and let me know with a very clear message. Sure enough, I called the branch as soon as they opened that day and when the manager checked the paperwork again she could see the discrepancy right away. Personally, I still find this kind of experience quite amazing.

On a much grander scale, you can hand over enormous, complicated and seemingly intractable problems to your intuition, intuitive mind, clairvoyant mind, creative mind, subconscious mind, higher mind – whatever you would like to call it – and it will work out the solution for you and deliver it to you clearly. All you need to do is engage with it again consciously and deliberately and learn to listen. Many inventors over the centuries have confessed that the breakthrough they had doggedly been pursuing only came to them after they gave up. After letting go of the task of trying to find the answer and make it happen from the level of conscious, thinking mind they found that their intuitive mind went to work on it automatically and showed the solution to them later, often when they least expected it.

The intuitive, creative mind does not work in a linear and rational manner. During our waking hours, when most of us are trying to control our minds and force it to perform in a certain way, we tend to do things in a step by step manner. This is considered to be more logical and 'right'. This approach can be very useful in certain fields where it is important to have clear records of events and information formatted in a way that most people could understand. The problem is that we have come to see information as knowledge and knowledge as wisdom, so we tend to revere the logical, linear way as the best way, leaving plenty of room for sceptics and cynics to denigrate anyone who does not or cannot operate effectively within that system. It is my personal belief, after years on my own path and of listening to the anguish of so many people, that forcing ourselves to live and think in this mechanical, inflexible way is one of the chief causes of so much of our anxiety and neuroses.

That poor old Little Voice in most people must be hoarse by now after years of trying to make itself heard above the clamour of all the fretting about the past, worrying about the future, going over and over old dramas and grievances, the doom and gloom on the news … not to mention all the things you are juggling about in that head of yours on a daily basis! The 'shopping list', as I like to call it, is full of all that monkey mind psychological gravel that never seems to stop tumbling around in your head. It gets in the way of the natural and much more subtle communications that can take place between your conscious mind, intuitive mind and that connection to the wisdom of All That Is.

Like Professor Einstein, I am content to let the 'how' of how this all happens remain a mystery. The human heart and Soul needs the mysterious to feed on and breathe life into our often sterile and angular world. Our Souls seek out the numinous and ineffable constantly. Whether you are an astronomer attempting to puzzle out the question of creation, a rabbi trying to explain to your congregation why good things happen to seemingly bad people and bad things happen to seemingly good people, or a quantum physicist who imagines that String Theory is going to be the one that finally explains what matter is made of, what do you tend to find at the end of your investigations? More mysteries! And many more questions needing answers than you had before you began. Isn't it time we stopped trying to dissect the unknowable and intangible and just started working with it instead? My Angels and Spirit Guides seem to think so. What's more, when you do start working with it, not only do you find that it is fun, useful, helpful and fulfilling, you also find that it is gentle, graceful, foolproof and has been there waiting to support you all along.

The *only* certainty that I have about the wonderful mystery that psychologists call the subconscious mind and that I like to call the Intuitive Mind, is that when you finally get around to acknowledging its existence and make the small effort required to engage with it, 'It' always responds.

CONNECTING WITH YOUR INTUITIVE MIND – A DIALOGUE

REQUIREMENTS: Peace and quiet.

OPTIONAL: Your journal and a pen.

TIME REQUIRED: 10 to 15 minutes

HOW OFTEN SHOULD I DO IT? Daily, or whenever you need some great guidance!

◆ Sit or lie down comfortably where you won't be disturbed for the time required. Take a few minutes to consider whatever it is you would like to communicate with your Intuitive Mind about.

◆ Contemplate your intention in this process. You, the conscious, thinking You, is going to call upon and communicate with your own Intuitive Mind.

◆ Give your Intuitive Mind a name if you like. Have fun choosing a name – it can be one that you like, one that means something special to you or simply the first name that pops into your head. If nothing comes straight away then use 'Intuitive Mind' as the name for now.

◆ Another enjoyable step can be to imagine what your Intuitive Mind would look like if it had a physical form. What would you like your Intuitive Mind to look like?

Note: this is a very creative process, allowing your imagination to form a picture of your Intuitive Mind for you brings the whole interaction to life. Our conscious minds associate things like name and appearance with identity, so basically, what you are doing is developing an identity for your Intuitive Mind that your conscious mind can relate to, rather than always relating to it as a vague 'it' or 'thing'. I call my Intuitive Mind Annabelle and to me she looks like a cheeky and spirited young woman with red, ringlet hair and gypsy-style clothing. Once your conscious mind, with its tendency to monkey around, has something more familiar to focus on it will be less inclined to distract you.

◆ Now there is nothing else left to do other than communicate. Talk to your Intuitive Mind in your head or out loud, just as you would talk to a caring and helpful friend. Clearly describe any problem or concern that you would like some assistance with. You can go into as much or as little detail as you wish. Your Intuitive Mind will get the gist.

◆ Ask your Intuitive Mind to clearly show or spell out to you what the solution is or what you need to do to help bring the solution about. If it is something you want, then ask your Intuitive Mind to help you achieve or receive your dream outcome. There is no right or wrong way to word it. Just talk to your Intuitive Mind as you would to someone who loves you, wants the best for you and can help you to create small miracles in your everyday life.

◆ When you are finished saying what you need to say, be sure to thank your Intuitive Mind and bid him or her farewell for now. It can all be very casual and friendly. There is no grand ceremony or protocol.

◆ Take a few moments to write down the name and description of your Intuitive Mind and a brief summary of whatever it was you spoke with them about.

◆ If you choose to do this process last thing at night as I prefer to do, then tuck yourself up and sleep well, secure in the knowledge that your requests are being taken care of and that the answers will come to you at the perfect time. Otherwise just continue on with your day, enjoy it, and let your Intuitive Mind take care of your requests. It will definitely report back to you!

After you have completed this process a few times you will have a good idea of what your Intuitive Mind likes to be called and what it looks like. So for all future dialogues you can just go straight into whatever it is you need to ask for or discuss. I say dialogue and discuss, because this process will definitely become interactive after some practice. Some people converse back and forth with their Intuitive Mind at the first attempt, but for most people, including me, it took a few rounds before I tuned into Annabelle's voice. Think of a radio station you have never listened to before. Just because you haven't heard it yet doesn't mean the sound isn't there, you simply need to find the right frequency and tune your equipment in.

As you become more experienced with this process your journal may not be necessary either. It is completely up to you. If you enjoy keeping a record of the things you asked for help with and would enjoy looking back on those entries, then by all means continue to make them. Just don't let the absence of a journal stop you; because you can easily have this kind of chat with your Intuitive Mind on the run. You may contact and communicate with your own personal Annabelle any time you like. After a while it becomes second nature to hand the mysteries of life over to your Intuitive Mind for sorting out, and once you become accustomed to whatever form of conversation works best for you and learn to listen to the responses, you will wonder how you ever did without it.

Many of my students and clients have found that the solution will come back in the form of a clear verbal message, a voice in your head, telling you what you need to do, be more aware of or whatever. You can specifically request that the answers be delivered to you in that way, so that you and your Intuitive Mind are clear on where you stand. It is great exercise for your intuition and clairvoyance – learning to listen out for that Little Voice, because when it comes to that particular voice you will be retraining yourself to listen not with your ears, but with your heart.

JOSIE'S EXPERIENCE

I had admired an American man who worked on the same floor of my building for a few months. We used to chat in the lift and sometimes shared a table in the local food court at lunchtime. He was always very friendly to me, enquiring about general aspects of my life and happy to make conversation. Over time he discovered that I was single and that we had quite a few interests in common. I longed for him to ask me out for a drink, but he never did, and I wondered if I should take the initiative.

Not wishing to make a fool of myself, I decided to consult my Intuitive Mind first by following the process BelindaGrace taught me. I completed this exercise just before going to bed and that night had the most amazing dream. In the dream I saw myself calling him from my mobile phone and asking him to meet me at the beach. Suddenly we were both at the location I had suggested and he looked so thrilled to be there with me. We even kissed passionately for a while! Then we walked and swam, enjoying each other's company. It was a lot of fun.

Next I found myself swimming alone and the water had become shallow and murky. I looked around for him and he was standing on the beach dressed in a suit. As I approached him he said he had to go because he had something important to do. I felt so deflated as our romantic get together had clearly come to an abrupt end.

When I woke from the dream a female sounding voice said clearly in my head "please wait" and I felt reassured, despite the disappointing outcome of the dream. I chose to interpret it as saying that it might be fun in the short term, but that there was something that was as yet unclear – murky – to me and that if I waded in I would be disappointed. I chose not to ask him out for a drink and find out more about him in the meantime.

A close friend of mine came to the rescue. She discovered that although he didn't wear a wedding ring he was in fact married. His wife and two children were in America and they were having a trial separation. Apparently he intended to visit them at Christmas but wasn't at all sure about the marriage or indeed what country he would be living in long term. My friend discovered that he did like me a great deal, but had thought it best not to lead me on in view of his complicated situation. He had done the right thing by just being friendly and I had saved myself a lot of potential embarrassment and even heartache.

For the next few months we continued to have our pleasant conversations in the lift and the food court, sharing stories about whatever we'd been up to recently. Then one day he told me he was going back to America indefinitely and wished me well; and I felt so glad that I had asked my Intuitive Mind for help.

JOSIE
AUSTRALIA

CHAPTER SEVEN

LEARNING TO TRUST YOUR INTUITION

All our progress is an unfolding, like a vegetable bud. You first have an instinct, then an opinion, then a knowledge as the plant has root, bud and fruit. Trust the instinct to the end though you can render no reason.

RALPH WALDO EMERSON
ESSAYIST AND POET
1803–1882

We might as well get this out of the way right at the beginning of this chapter; the guidance, suggestions, inspirations and solutions that will come to you via your intuitive and clairvoyant abilities are not going to come running at you and hit you over the head. The Universe is an amazingly subtle place and we have filled our lives with almost constant noise, busy-ness and distraction. Try to imagine for a moment what life would have been like before the widespread availability of electricity and the invention of the car – no televisions or radios giving off their constant babble, no computers, internet or playstations, no traffic noise. Step back a further 150 years to the days before the industrial revolution. No trains, no machines, no factories.

Now I am not trying to imply that people were more connected to their intuitions in those days, but the quieter lifestyle must, at the very least, have been more conducive to conversation, reflection and contemplation. Certainly we know that many philosophers and poets from those eras were the rock stars of their day. Who but the smallest minority of people talks philosophy these days? And when was the last time you bought and read a collection of poetry written by a contemporary poet?

The point I am making is this – your Little Voice is constantly being drowned out by what we regard as 'normal life'. But normal is a relative term. Go and talk to someone who lives in a country where only one household in the neighbourhood might have a small television, where a rural existence is still the norm after centuries. To those people the 24-hour-a-day bombardment of advertising, information, entertainment and relentless invasion of all forms of media into our lives would be considered far from normal. Every external distraction takes you away from your inner life and can diminish your connection to it. So what is the solution? That's simple – balance.

Very few of us would be truly willing to leave all we have behind and go live in a hut somewhere. There is no reason at all why you shouldn't enjoy all that the 21st century has to offer, as long as you also make time for some peace, quiet and meditation in any of its forms. Any genuinely quiet and restful time is healing and harmonising for the Soul and will offer up the chance to repair the bridges between your outer and your inner worlds. It's not about going to extremes or denouncing one or the other, it's about embracing the whole spectrum of our modern lifestyles.

One of the reasons that your intuition will speak to you at two or three in the morning is because that is the only time of the day that your mind is reasonably still. It is the only time that the subtle Little Voice can break through. The good news is however – and this is very good news – that just because communications from the All That Is are subtle, doesn't mean that they aren't clear or reliable. In fact, once you become reacquainted with the art of listening, you will be delighted at how clear the prompts, reminders, nudges and messages are.

It's all a matter of a little patience, a little practice and yes, a little peace and quiet every day. Next time you are preparing a meal, reading a book, doing the housework or even reading your emails, try turning the television and the radio off and go about your activities surrounded by quiet. Even then, when you are engaged in some kind of activity, your Little Voice will have more of a chance to surface.

GERALDINE'S EXPERIENCE

One day, not that long ago, I was rushing around as usual trying to do three things at once. I was due to meet a couple of friends at the station so we could all travel together to a musical we had tickets for in the city. I was running so late and I knew my friends would be really annoyed with me if I caused us to miss the train and the beginning of the show.

I had bought a new kitten a couple of weeks before. She had plenty of toys to amuse her while I was out so I popped her food bowl on the floor, patted her goodbye and raced out the front door. As I was locking up a voice inside my head said to me clearly 'go back inside and go to the sunroom'. My immediate reaction was 'No! I am going to miss the train, I can't be late or the girls will be furious!' but the voice persisted with the same message. I stood for a few more seconds arguing with this voice and telling it why I couldn't go back inside, but it never let up. In fact, despite my rising panic about the time, this voice had a strong and calming effect on me.

I raced back inside and all the way through to the back of my house to the sunroom. There I got a huge shock because in the minute or so that it had taken me to proceed from patting my kitten to locking the front door she had gone to the sunroom and become completely entangled in the Venetian blind cord. She was actually being choked by it and her struggling was only making things worse. She was giving out a strangled cry and was very frightened.

I untangled her quickly and soothed her. In that moment I was not at all concerned about the time or the musical. I loved my kitten and I wanted to make sure she was fine. While I sat there on the sofa cradling her, I rummaged around in my handbag for my mobile phone, intending to call the girls and apologise. I wanted to tell them to go on ahead, to not miss the start of the show and I would catch them up.

To my surprise there was a message on my phone but I hadn't heard it ring, I had forgotten to reset it from silent. The message was from one of my friends saying that she had decided to drive us all to the theatre and that they would come pick me up at 6.30pm, which was now about 15 minutes away. Driving in, she said, would be quicker, so we wouldn't have to leave so early.

Not only did my intuition prompt me to go back and save my kitten's life, but everything else fell into place as well. I truly feel that my friend's last minute decision to drive was not mere coincidence, but pure serendipity organised on my behalf by this elegant and awesome Universe.

Geraldine Y.
Sydney, Australia

Geraldine's kitten survived thanks to Geraldine's ability to hear her Little Voice and her *willingness to act on its instructions*. Geraldine has been meditating for a couple of years and recently completed the first term of one of my courses. Her meditation practice has been as sporadic and frustrating as most other busy people find it, but she always goes back to it eventually, even if she can only spare a few minutes for herself. You may have also noticed in the telling of her story that she experienced a feeling of calm along with the message itself, despite the frantic state of her monkey mind.

Finally, the key thing to take focus on is the content of the message itself. It was simple and very straightforward, giving her clear directions of what to do, not *why* she should do it. Perhaps if Geraldine's Little Voice had told her that the kitten was choking to death on the blind cord she would have become even more stressed and dropped her keys, fumbled the lock or something else that would have wasted precious seconds. The message was clear and direct because it needed to be. In that moment she didn't actually need to know the reason, she just had to take action quickly and the results were perfect.

But this is the part that can trip you up when you are only just getting reacquainted with your inner guidance. Divine guidance is always very efficient and simple. It is not the Universe trying to test you or be cryptic, which is the way many people choose to see it, but rather it is simply giving you the essential information that you need to get the job done. So this is where the trust element begins to really show up. The more confident you become in recognising true guidance, discerning it amongst the general chitter-chatter of your mind, the more confident you will become about acting upon it. The more you will trust it. Your Little Voice doesn't have an issue with trust, so it just takes it on face value that you have each other's best interests at heart.

The questions people always ask me when I talk about receiving messages from my Angels and Spirit Guides, or being given guidance by my Little Voice, are: "But how do you know it's not just your mind making it up? How do you know your not just thinking those words yourself? How do you know when to trust it?" They are good questions and the next exercise will show you how to recognise the difference between useful intuitive guidance and your conscious mind trying to figure it out.

EXERCISE FIVE

RECOGNISING AND TRUSTING INTUITIVE GUIDANCE

REQUIREMENTS: Your journal and a pen.
Peaceful surroundings so you can relax and concentrate.

OPTIONAL: Very soft, gentle music, a candle or incense.
Anything that helps you create a meditative atmosphere.

TIME REQUIRED: 15 to 20 minutes.

HOW OFTEN SHOULD I DO THIS? At least once as the complete exercise detailed below. Then feel free to add any experiences to your journal as they come to mind and take a minute or two to sit with that feeling whenever you can. For those of you who are keen to develop your skills quickly, I recommend completing the whole process once a month.

◆ **Part one – journal exercise** – Make a note of some of the times in your life when you didn't follow your intuition and regretted it. Write down anything you know or you feel you missed out on by not following that urge, feeling or hunch. For example – you went out for a drink after work on Friday night because that is what you always do. It's expected that you will tag along with everyone else from the office. You didn't really want to go, but you talked yourself into it, despite the fact that you had a strong feeling you should go home. When you arrive home a couple of hours later there is a note under your door from a friend who had popped by to visit hoping to find you in. You feel annoyed with yourself and disappointed that you weren't home to see your friend.

Take your time and write down as many examples as you can think of.

◆ Now make a list of all the times you did follow one of those inexplicable, even illogical, hunches or urges and what the positive outcome was. Write down all of the positive things that happened to or for you as a result of following that hunch. For example – you are applying for a job that you know hundreds of another people will also apply for. You have strong feeling that if you write you application and CV by hand and format it more like a personal letter it will stand out from the crowd of dry, impersonal applications. Not only do you get an interview, you are offered the job. Naturally you are well qualified, but your new employer tells you that she loved your application because she was able to get a sense of you as a real person. Your application stood out and made her want to meet you. Congratulations!

Take your time and write down as many examples as you
can think of.

◆ **Part two – a meditation** – Choosing from one of the
experiences you have written down, close your eyes
and allow yourself to remember how you *felt* when you
suppressed your intuitive urge. Take yourself back to that
exact moment in time and replay it, tuning in to how you
felt.

Allow those feelings to come up again. How did you feel
as your working day was ending and you knew that you
would all be going downstairs for a drink as usual? What
sort of dialogue was going on in your mind? Did you have
a knot of anxiety in your solar plexus area wishing you
could just tell your colleagues you were going straight
home tonight, but dreaded their reaction? How hard
did you have to work to push down the feelings you had
about doing what was right for you and talking yourself
into doing what you believed was expected of you? What
were you feeling as you sat in the bar wishing you could
be home instead?

◆ Stay with the feelings of the whole experience, including
how you felt when you realised that your decision to
overrule your intuition had other consequences.

◆ Stay with the feelings that you had during that time.
Allow them to sink in and commit them to your mind and

body-memory. Then create an intention and promise yourself to be more aware of and to respond to those signals in the future.

Note: 'Body-memory' is an incredibly powerful thing and is part of the intuitive process. A second or two before you become consciously aware of an intuitive thought, idea or solution, your body will let you know what is going on. If you are flushed with a feeling of happiness, reassured by a feeling of calmness or instantly warned by a feeling of anxiety or fear then you need to at least stop for a moment and consider those messages. What tends to happen though is that we ignore or override them and plough on regardless, partly out of habit and partly because of the pressure of all the 'shoulds' and 'have to's' in our minds.

Reconnecting with your body's response to the situation you are meditating on and committing that to body-memory is every bit as helpful as committing the memory of what you learned to mind memory for future reference. Becoming aware of your physical responses as they happen and taking a moment to consider their importance is a great way to expand on your intuitive and clairvoyant abilities and will make it more natural to pay attention to them next time they show up. Again, this is another example of the law of the jungle. Long before we could read, write or speak, we were feeling, intuitive creatures who had to trust our instincts in order to survive.

◆ Then, choosing an experience where you did follow your intuition, close your eyes and relive how you felt when you got that positive urge and acted on it.

- Did you feel a nervous excitement about the idea of creating an application that would look and read differently to all the others? Maybe you even had a strong sense that the job would be yours. Maybe you even had a thought like "wow, that's a brilliant idea, I wonder what made me think of doing it that way?"

- Take as much time as you need to remember any tug-of-war that you might have had with yourself about stepping outside the square. How did you feel when you finally decided to do things your way?

- Sit with all the feelings and memories from that time, including the deeper knowing that would have been there somewhere that said "I have to do it my way because this is who I am, this is authentic. Therefore if this job really is the right one for me then I know I will get it."

- Lock those feelings into your conscious awareness and body-memory for future reference, creating an intention to respond to them even more confidently next time they come.

- Repeat this exercise whenever you remember any other situations like these from the past. It is worth working with all the experiences that you can remember eventually, because each one will contain its own subtle nuances and their own unique mixture of 'red light' or 'green light' emotions.

In no time at all you will develop a memory bank of intuitive wisdom and become more comfortable with the languages that your intuitive and clairvoyant guidance uses. It is important to understand the Universe doesn't speak or have a preference for English, or any other human language for that matter, and will often use words only as an addition to feelings, urges and instincts. We are much more instinctual and spiritual beings than we usually choose to recognise, and your intuition, Divine Guidance, Angels and so on will use these clear and immediate pathways to communicate with you.

Finally, an interesting point about 'gut-feel'. Did you know that when the fetus is forming in the womb the cluster of cells that develop into the nerves that make up the brain and the cluster of cells that make up the nerves of the solar plexus start out as one bundle of cells altogether? This means that our solar plexus or 'gut' is literally our second brain. A simpler, more visceral perceptive organ that responds to changes in energy, vibration, atmosphere and feelings seconds before the more sophisticated upper brain has had time to process the same information.

TARA'S EXPERIENCE

Tara was keen to meet with a very famous musician who was in Australia on a concert tour. She had a ticket to his show, but had been unable to secure a backstage pass. Undeterred, Tara had a strong feeling that she would be able to get backstage somehow, and held on to that positive feeling and thought.

A friend of mine was unexpectedly in town and he invited me to come and have coffee at his hotel. When I arrived, my friend welcomed me, and without realising that I was actually hoping to meet this famous musician, he told me that the musician was staying at the same hotel.

Within seconds of being given that information I had a strong feeling to go and walk through the restaurant at the other side of the hotel. It was a strong feeling in my solar plexus, not a pain or a cramp, more like a rush or intensifying of energy.

As I hesitated for a few seconds to think about it, a strong thought came into my mind that said "Just go!" As my friend walked in the direction of the café to secure a table there, I walked towards the restaurant instead. Sure enough, the musician I had wanted to meet was sitting in the restaurant, by himself. Suddenly feeling a little awkward, I noticed the door for the powder room a short distance away. I walked across the restaurant, went into the powder room and took a few seconds to compose myself. I resolved to talk to this famous man on my way out; which is exactly what I did.

Not only did I find him to be very friendly, we had a lovely chat and he was delighted to hear that I would be at his concert that night. He quipped "well, at least someone is coming!" He invited me backstage and when I arrived at the box office to pick up the passes, I found that he had also left tickets for much better seats. It turned out to be a fantastic night thanks to my intuition.

TARA P.
SYDNEY, AUSTRALIA

Wouldn't you love to allow your feelings to guide you into wonderful situations like that? Well, you can. Starting right now with this exercise. Learning to recognise and respond to the languages of your intuition, clairvoyance, heart and Soul is the passport to magical experiences every day of your life. Once again, Tara's Little Voice didn't say to her "go and walk through the restaurant because the person you want to meet is sitting there". She got the strong feeling in her solar plexus first, then the words "just go" when she hesitated. Start practising now so that you can discover the special qualities of the way your Divine Guidance communicates with you.

CHAPTER EIGHT

DISCOVERING WHO YOU ARE

So when I talk about having good hearing, I don't mean just listening, but listening to yourself. When I talk about good eyesight, I don't mean just looking, but looking at yourself.

CHUANG TZU
CHINESE PHILOSOPHER
360–275 BC

In order for you to live a life that you find inspiring and worthwhile you need to have a good sense of who you are. Why? Because when you know who you are, what you want from life becomes a lot clearer; and when you know what you actually want to do with your life and get from it, you can set about creating those things and using them as a way of expressing yourself.

Being authentic, living your truth and living with meaning and purpose are all ways of saying to yourself and the world 'I know who I am and this is how I choose to express myself'. When you are unclear about who you are it's a bit like being rudderless on the high seas. You get dragged around by the currents and tides, tossed about in life's storms and end up washed up on somebody else's shores wondering how on earth you got there.

Maybe you know who you are in some ways but not in others. It is very common, for instance, for someone to know that they want to be married or to be a parent, but to have no idea how to be fulfilled in their work. A common fantasy that attaches to that particular conundrum is a dream of winning the lottery or some such, which is just another way of expressing a desire to escape. There is no reason why you shouldn't or can't win the lottery, but until that happens, wouldn't it be nice to be fulfilled in your work anyway? Even if I won the lottery tomorrow, I know I would still continue to do what I do, which is a marvellous situation to be in because either way I'm happy.

You may have already noticed that the word 'authentic' made an appearance in the last chapter. It isn't always the easiest word to relate to, although it gets bandied about quite a bit these days. Maybe you would prefer to think of being authentic or living an authentic life as being real, down to earth, true to yourself, following your heart, self-aware or something along those lines. Whatever you choose to call it, it's all about knowing who you are and expressing your uniqueness in the way you approach and live your life. We may well be eternal, with Souls that live on for ever and reincarnate in many different forms, but the real point of life is to live it and enjoy it now, and being real helps you to do just that.

Knowing who you are and living from that awareness as much as possible every day also has an amazing impact on your intuitive and clairvoyant capacity. Or is it the other way around? In my experience it is a wonderful cycle that feeds itself and keeps growing. When you embark on the journey of uncovering and connecting with who you really are, many other elements of your life begin to fall into place. Your vibration or frequency starts to change and you then start to attract experiences and things that are a match for your new way of being.

When you are living your life from a place of self awareness you are on your path and the Universe loves nothing more than a person who is embracing their own unique qualities. My Angels and Guides are always saying to people, 'there is no such thing as right or wrong, just experience and experiment.'

Perhaps it is time for you to stop trying so hard to get it right, and stop worrying about getting it wrong. What if you simply gave yourself permission to get out there and embrace the life you have?

The quest to understand ourselves and discover who we are is Universal and a journey worth embarking on. So here are some simple ways to help you take those first, important steps. Some of you will already be some way along the path, so this exercise will help you to refine your self awareness and to acknowledge some of the dusty corners of your inner world that haven't been explored yet.

For those of you who feel you have a healthy sense of self, I would encourage you to give this exercise a go anyway; you might surprise yourself. Sometimes getting to know yourself is as much a matter of prioritising what is important and meaningful to you as is uncovering these things in the first place. Even the most aware person goes through various phases and stages in life where one area may recede into the background and another may become more important. An obvious example might be the transition from full-time motherhood to career woman once your children have grown up and left home. Each scenario demands that you know yourself and what you want from quite different perspectives.

In a nutshell you could put it this way. You are what

you stand for, you are what you believe in, you are what you choose to act upon, you are what you choose to think about, you are your values and what is important to you, you are what you choose to commit to, you are what you feel, you are what makes your heart sing and you are what you have brought in with you. For too many people most of these elements of themselves are vague, subject to the opinions and approval of others, deliberately suppressed or even completely obscure. How are you supposed to live a life of inspiration, meaning and purpose if you don't know the answers to at least some of these most fundamental questions? Knowing who you are, or at least taking steps along the path of self discovery, is the foundation of living the kind of life you truly desire.

UNDERSTANDING WHO YOU REALLY ARE

REQUIREMENTS: Your journal and a pen.

OPTIONAL: Gentle music to create a nice mood.

TIME REQUIRED: 15 to 20 minutes

HOW OFTEN SHOULD I DO THIS? Once a fortnight until you feel you have a good level of self awareness.
Every six to twelve months thereafter.

Part one – journal exercise

◆ Take a clean page in your journal and write the heading 'Understanding Who I Really Am' and underline it. This helps to set your intention.

The way you lay this exercise out will depend on your own personal style and the way you like doing things. One excellent method is to divide your pages up into columns or sections, each with a sub-heading of their own. Such as 'Things I believe in', 'Things I stand for', 'Things that I am committed to', 'What is important to me', 'My Values', 'The things that make my heart sing are'. When it comes to thoughts and feelings, you may wish to head your page 'Feelings I consistently experience' or 'Feelings I consistently have', 'Thoughts I consistently or frequently think', 'Things I often think about'.

If you find this approach too methodical or limiting then use your open page and write down what comes to you in whatever order it comes. You don't have to put your realisations into categories. Only do it that way if you feel it would help you. Please note, you can start out with a page of random realisations and then streamline them into groups later if you wish.

- Stay with this part of the exercise until you come up with at least five expressions of yourself. Do not critique or judge them, this is a process of revealing, unearthing and discovering, not a process of getting it right!

- Keep writing all the ideas, realisations and revelations that come to you. If it really starts to flow don't block it off. Write as fast as you can! Then, when you have written all you can or all you want to for now, re-read your list once or twice and notice what jumps out at you.

Note: It is very enlightening at this point in the exercise to notice where the real you clearly shows up in your day-to-day life and where you know you hide or suppress yourself. You may also be amazed to find that you regularly suppress some areas of your Being and hadn't even realised you were doing it until now. It might seem like you have been playing the role of a character in a movie or play that has been directed by someone or something other than yourself. In the next part of this journey you are going to be the main character in your own story again, but this time you will also be seated firmly in the director's chair!

Part two – the whole-self visualisation

◆ Take a moment to collect your thoughts and to make sure that you are sitting comfortably.

◆ Close your eyes and visualise yourself going about your life throughout the course of a normal week; for example going to work, fitness or sport, any course or class you normally attend, family activities, socialising on the weekend and so on. Create a movie in your mind of what it would look like if someone filmed a week of your life exactly the way it is now.

◆ The difference with this film footage however is that as you are visualising it and following the story you can feel all the feelings that the main character – YOU – is feeling as you go about your day. Notice those feelings as they come up, but don't get stuck in any of them, just keep the movie rolling and follow the story.

◆ After a few minutes of the movie about the way things are now, start to allow some of the expressions of yourself that you wrote down in your journal to seep in to your behaviours in this visualisation of your life.

For instance, you may have written down that staying fit and healthy all your life is really important to you, but then the beginning of your visualisation showed you putting off fitness activities or eating fast food on the run because you let other things get on top of you or take up too much of your time. Maybe you wrote down that you value quality time with your children, yet your initial visualisation shows that you never speak up when somebody else calls in sick and your boss asks you to work late to cover for them.

◆ As you make the transition in your visualisation from the way things are now to a visualisation of a whole and complete you creating your life, you can direct these things to change. Visualise yourself saying to your parents 'Yes I am still coming over for dinner tomorrow night, but I will be arriving at 7.30 pm instead of 6 pm because I am going to a yoga class first.' They may throw their arms up and wail about eating dinner so late, but remember, if your life was a movie you would want to be the director, right? So in your visualisation you let them complain for a moment and then calmly state "Well, now that you mention it I would prefer a lighter meal anyway; instead of a roast and potatoes why don't we just have a salad and I will bring some fruit for dessert." Then visualise yourself going to the yoga class and arriving at the time of your choosing.

Next you might direct your movie to the work situation, and instead of the old vision of you sitting there fuming but not saying anything, you visualise yourself leaving work at a decent time and not feeling guilty about it. Your boss may look exasperated as you wave goodbye, but if there are any snide comments or objections visualise yourself dealing with the situation from your very aware self. 'I am sorry you have so much work left to do before you can leave, boss, but I have covered for the others so many times already. Quality time with my children is very important to me and if I get home too late all I get to do is tuck them into bed. I'm their father after all and I want to be there for them. See you tomorrow.'

◆ Visualise your entire week, making all the necessary adjustments as you go and allow yourself to feel the feelings of the star of your show – YOU. Notice how empowered, confident and happy you feel as you go through your life speaking your truth, doing things that make you feel good and setting healthy boundaries with the people in your life.

◆ Finish your visualisation by saying to yourself in your mind or out loud "I am whole and complete, I love myself and I am enough" at least three times or as many times as you like.

♦ Open your eyes, jot down anything significant that came to you during your visualisation process and pat yourself on the back for a job well done.

This simple process can be so incredibly exciting and inspiring. Going through the steps of putting into words the ways of being that express and represent you is an empowering way to get you on your highest path. Then the added step of visualising yourself making the transition into wholeness is a way of bringing the pieces of the puzzle back together and settling them back into place. It is an important rehearsal for taking real action in your life and sets a whole new stage for the way things are going to be from now on. You are coming back into alignment with your true and authentic self. This is an evolutionary process, so there is no final destination, no end to the depth of who you are. Your connection with yourself and who you truly are can continue to widen and deepen forever.

Eventually you will be directing and starring in your own life all of the time and finding it easier to notice when you start to drift off track. Instead of getting lost in the brambles of a misdirected life for months or years at a time, you will gradually reclaim your ability to steer yourself straight again quickly and with the minimum of fuss. Sometimes life does seem to take over, and that's okay, there is nothing right or wrong, just experience and experiment. So use this process to check in with yourself regularly to make sure you are happy with the path you are on. Each time you make an improvement and fill out the wholeness of your self, your confidence and self esteem will grow. This in turn makes it easier to make other improvements further down the line. Congratulations, you are on your way to a better relationship with the only person you will ever spend your whole life with. Twenty-four hours a day, seven days a week you are with yourself, so, you might as well have a wonderful understanding of who you are so you can enjoy the company!

BRAD'S EXPERIENCE

The funny and fantastic thing about doing, saying or thinking about something that is a real and authentic expression of who I am is that I both connect with myself and forget about myself at the same time.

The level of self that I connect with is bigger than the 'me' of my ordinary needs, wants and concerns and yet it does not neglect or disdain those things. I know that those things are easy to deal with and I am in the flow.

The level of self that I forget about is the part of me that wants to believe that I am separate from everything and everyone, the level of my mind that keeps me limited and small.

When I am being the real me everything flows nicely. Working takes on the quality of vocation, errands and chores become enjoyable tasks and living becomes an honour and a gift. I forget my tendency to feel pressured by time because I am fully focused in the moment and living in the here and now.

If I lose this feeling or get jolted out of it unexpectedly I regroup with a quick Whole-Self visualisation or by going back to my journal, re-reading my notes and sometimes adding more. That is my anchor, my centre and I love to revisit it. I love knowing that it is there for me to come back to any time I like.

BRAD J.
IDAHO, USA

CHAPTER NINE

AUTOMATIC WRITING – DIVINE GUIDANCE FROM YOUR INTUITIVE MIND

Intuition becomes increasingly valuable in the new information-based society, precisely because there is no such data.

JOHN NAISBITT
BORN 1929
BESTSELLING AUTHOR OF *MEGATRENDS*

Your Intuitive Mind (IM) is permanently connected to a source of wisdom, guidance and knowing that far exceeds any amount of knowledge and information you could absorb with your thinking mind or brain. When you access this connection in a practical manner you can receive information from this source to assist you in everyday life. No question is too small or trivial, nor could any question be too difficult or large. When you ask your IM to go and find you the answer it will do so; and once again, all you need to do is train yourself to listen.

After all these years I still find that Automatic Writing is one of the most powerful and effective ways to connect with Divine Guidance. Not only does it give your IM a clear instruction to bring you the advice you need, it strengthens that connection every time you undertake the practice. In my first book *You Are Clairvoyant – Developing the Secret Skill We All Have* I use the analogy of clearing out a disused pipe. When you first turn on a tap that hasn't had water flow through it for a long time the water will sputter and come out in fits and starts, often being murky and full of rust. After regular use though, the water will start to flow smoothly and cleanly again and be as good as new.

It's the same with Automatic Writing. If you haven't exercised your connection to your IM for a while then your channel may be a bit blocked and your connection a little rusty, but not to worry. Unlike solid objects such as a tap and pipe, your channel never deteriorates beyond repair and with practice and a little TLC you will be communicating with your IM again in no time.

Over the last two years or so my Angels and Spirit Guides have given me a very important and profound question to use for myself and with my students and clients. It is *the* question to ask when you truly want some guidance. This question has been specially designed to make it possible for an answer to come through which is for your highest good. What the Angels and Guides have often noticed in the past if that a lot of people tend to ask loaded or biased questions, either because they deliberately want to manipulate the answer or because their view of what is possible is quite limited and their expectations may be too low.

The nature of this question makes it a powerful invocation and invitation. The former because you are making it clear to the Universe that you are willing to do your part to bring your desires to fruition; and the latter because it acknowledges that so much more is possible than we can imagine. This question acknowledges that we are co-creators in our own lives working with both the steps we need to take on a practical, physical level and the sheer unlimited magic of the All That Is. Here in this exercise I will share that question with you and suggest various different forms you can put it into to best suit your situation.

MESSAGES FROM YOUR INTUITIVE MIND

REQUIREMENTS: Your journal and a pen. Peace and quiet.

OPTIONAL: Soft music, candles, incense. Anything you like to create a pleasant mood.

TIME REQUIRED: 10 to 15 minutes.

HOW OFTEN SHOULD I DO THIS? Whenever you have a question you would like to ask.

◆ Sit quietly for a minute and allow yourself to relax. Consider your simple intention – you are going to ask your Intuitive Mind a question and write down the answer in your journal.

◆ If you are not completely clear on what you would like to ask please take a moment to refine the nature of your question.

Note: You will find it a great deal easier to receive clear and useful guidance if you ask for guidance on one topic at a time. Questions that try to cover a number of situations, problems, needs or desires all in one go will become too complicated. One question, one topic. That is the best approach.

- Close your eyes and recall whatever you already know about your Intuitive Mind just as you would when remembering the qualities and characteristics of a close friend. Go over what you have already learned and noticed about your IM such as his or her name and appearance. Then speak to your IM either in your mind or out loud: "Dear *Name/Intuitive Mind*, I am going to ask you a question that is very important to me; I request and am ready to receive your wisdom and guidance. Thank you for your help and for bringing the answers to me".

- Now write this question:

  "What do I need to do or not do, start or stop, embrace or let go of in order to lead a happier and more fulfilling life?"

- This next step is very important. You must write down anything and everything that comes to you without censoring, correcting or judging it. Please write down whatever comes in whatever form it does. Some people will get single words or short, succinct statements. Others will get rambling or repetition. Sometimes you may even start to write a rhyme or poem.

  If you have something to write immediately, that is terrific, but be patient with yourself if it takes a little longer. Keep re-reading the question if that helps until a reply comes into your mind.

Note: some people imagine that your hand just takes over and starts to write as though it is beyond your control. Automatic Writing is not like that. It's not about going into some sort of trance! This exercise is about opening the doorway to your Intuitive Mind and your natural wellspring of inspiration so that it can flow to you in the form of words that you can write down, re-read later and benefit from.

When you tap into this level of higher awareness or intelligence there can be a sense of urgency to get it all onto the page, sometimes it's as though you almost can't write quickly enough. At other times the inspiration will come through in a gentle, lilting way that can feel very nurturing. Practice is the key here, and every time you engage with your IM in this way you will experience another of the myriad ways that it can communicate back to you. Remember, we are trying to capture something that is infinite and format it into the relatively limned framework of language. Be patient with yourself and the process and give your own personal style time to develop.

◆ When you truly feel you have written down all that is going to come to you for now, finish your session by writing: "Dear *Name/Intuitive Mind,* thank you, I am very grateful for all your help. Please bring me all that I desire and require in its best and highest possible form." Finish your session with this statement of gratitude even if you wrote nothing this time around.

- Take a moment to sit with and notice how you feel now that you have put that question forward and committed to receiving the highest form of response.

The question I have given you is a wonderful way to help you stay on track in a general way. To help you live "a more fulfilling life". In fact, because our lives are always changing and evolving, I recommend that you use the original form of this question once or twice a year. The answers can vary greatly and will form a wonderful reflection of you, your journey and whatever it is you need to focus upon most at the time of asking.

There will also be times when you can benefit enormously from tailoring this question to specific concerns or situations. I have provided a few examples, but as long as you retain the essential structure of the question and use the statement of gratitude at the end you can invent as many versions of your own as you like. The magic of this question and answer approach lies in the fact that you are accessing your Intuitive Mind, acknowledging its connection to infinite wisdom and its ability to help you, *combined with* a declaration of your willingness to do your share. That way, you are actively putting forward your intention to be a co-creator in your life and affirming to the Universe "I am willing to meet you in the middle so we can work together" What could be more powerful than that?

Variations on *The Question* –

◆ What do I need to do or not do, start or stop, embrace or let go of in order to attract my Soulmate?

◆ What do I need to do or not do, start or stop, embrace or let go of in order to improve my health – recover from my current illness?

◆ What do I need to do or not do, start or stop, embrace or let go of in order to get a better job – improve my income – pay off all my debts?

◆ What do I need to do or not do, start or stop, embrace or let go of in order to improve my relationship with my spouse, partner, employer, friend etc?

◆ What do I need to do or not do, start or stop, embrace or let go of in order to help me realise my dream of doing or becoming …?

Another word on perseverance and practice. This is a simple and effective process, but like all things in life you may not attain gold medal level without a little practice. My promise to you is that if you persevere with this you will get some positive results. Take your mind back to Kerryn, the 'runt of the litter' in one of my courses who is now practising as a Clairvoyant Healer; or Mark, who never gave up no matter how many times he tripped himself up. It is very important that you don't fall prey to the false promises of our quick-fix society and become despondent just because your first attempt doesn't turn out to be a treatise on enlightenment. You will get your helpful communications from your Intuitive Mind by using this method over and over again. Practice not only makes perfect; it will help you to rebuild your intuitive muscle so that it will be strong and function well for you whenever you need it.

Helping a Friend.

If you really want to exercise and strengthen your courage muscles you can also ask your Intuitive Mind for guidance and information that will assist others. If you have a friend or family member who could really use some help, you and your IM could be just what they need.

Sit and talk with this person and discuss their dilemma so that you are clear as to what the problem is. Let them know that you can only ask a question about one topic at a time. Use the question in its original form for excellent, all-round guidance, or if you prefer to make the question more specific then make it direct and simple like any of the above examples. Sometimes you may need to be creative, for example, perhaps your friend isn't very happy with his or her current job and has been looking around for a while. He or she hasn't had any definite offers from a new employer yet but he or she feels confident that it wouldn't take him or her long to secure another role in a new company. How would you put that into the format we have been using?

You could try posing the question this way –

What does (friend's name) need to do or not do, start or stop, embrace or let go of in order to have a job he or she finds enjoyable and fulfilling?

Keep working on the wording of the question until it feels good for both of you and fulfils the criteria of how to format this question. Every other step is the same. Set your intention, tune in to your IM, write the question down first and then write down whatever information comes to you. Don't judge it or worry about whether or not it will make sense to your friend. You are doing him or her a favour, doing your best to help out and it is up to them, as the final recipient of the message, to interpret what it means to him or her.

When making the gratitude statement thank your IM for the help and information it has brought your friend and ask that your friend receive all that she or he requires and desires. Well done and good on you for being willing to help.

The following information was written for me by a one day workshop student whom I paired up with to do this exact same exercise. I found this information very interesting and accurate, and I was happy to take on the advice of my student's Intuitive Mind.

What does BelindaGrace need to do or not do, start or stop, embrace or let go of in order to lead a happier and more fulfilling life?

'Stop! Listen to your Guides. You can have everything you want in your life. Do what is important to do for your long-term good. What really makes your heart sing? You love to do so many different things, you thrive on variety, but you can also dissipate your energy by heading in too many directions. So hold your space and really sit with your goals and aspirations at this time. This is a time just for you. The decisions you make at this time will affect your life for the next few years, so ask your Guides and Angels to show you the best way. Importantly, look at everything you do not want to do, everything that might not be fun and won't make your soul sing. It's a beautiful time for you and you are up there riding the waves.

Keep on going. Don't give up, only you put up the barriers to the things you believe you can't have. Hold those dreams, Belinda. Hold them and allow yourself to have them.'

CHAPTER TEN

LOOKING AT THE WORLD THROUGH NEW EYES

The real voyage of discovery consists not in seeking new landscapes but in having new eyes.

MARCEL PROUST
AUTHOR
1871–1922

I decided to include a chapter about this topic in this book a few months ago. The catalyst for the idea came to me as I sat listening to a client of mine telling me about her life. It was her first consultation; she was 23 and had only been living in Australia for two years after moving here from the United Kingdom. As it turned out, she also lived within walking distance of one of Sydney's most beautiful beaches.

For the next half hour, this lass, who was young enough to be my daughter, proceeded to tell me how dull and uninteresting her life was. How every day was pretty much the same and that her weekends were no great cause for excitement either because all she ever did was shop, clean the house and go out with a few friends. When I asked her if she liked living so close to the beach she shrugged her shoulders and replied 'Yeah, it's alright, I guess.'

I asked her about her job. It seemed to me that she had a career that at least had the potential to be interesting, as the personal assistant to the MD of a well known American film studio. She worked in the busy heart of the city, often got to see hit movies well before they were released to cinemas and had regular brushes with well known, creative and interesting people. Her response to that enquiry was that every day was pretty much the same. She said she knew what was going to happen every day and therefore it was boring!?! To be honest, by this point in the conversation

I didn't know whether or not to feel sorry for her or grab her by the shoulders and shake her. She was absolutely in earnest, she meant every word.

It struck me that this was a tragedy. How many people in poor and war-torn countries would give anything to have the kind of upbringing and opportunities she had enjoyed? She felt uninspired and unexcited about her life. Nothing she could think of doing held any great prospect for her. She was, she said, just going through the motions.

Now you might think that this was an extreme case. But I am regularly shocked and saddened by similar comments from many of the men and women who come to see me. Thankfully this kind of malaise will only affect one or two areas of most people's lives; but whichever way you look at it, it is still a heavy weight to carry around. I believe it is actually a form of depression, and perhaps for younger generations it is also a result of living in a society that pretends that instant gratification is healthy, when it is actually no more than an illusion.

Through the work that my Angels, Spirit Guides and I do with my clients we can tackle this kind of despondency. By reviewing and releasing past lives in which a certain experience may have given rise to this particular attitude or belief system, connecting the client with their own Angels and Spirit Guides so that they feel supported, and balancing their chakras and channel they can reconnect to the guidance of their own clairvoyant and intuitive mind.

All of these things help enormously and I have seen many lives turned completely around, which is very gratifying indeed.

Not surprisingly, while writing this chapter, I felt a strong urge to ask my Angels and Spirit Guides what they would like to say on the subject of enjoying our precious lives, because their input and guidance has always been a huge source of inspiration for me.

After sitting quietly and allowing myself to tune in, the voice that came through most clearly was that of Kuthumi, a marvellous spiritual being whom I communicate with regularly and who has been of enormous help to me, my clients and students over the years. Here is what Kuthumi had to say:

It is very important for all living beings to take responsibility for how they view life and what they create. You cannot go through life expecting the world to excite you. Humankind has proven over and over again that they can become bored with anything and everything no matter how novel, original or intriguing it may first appear. Every day you can generate your own sense of wonder and excitement; for no matter how powerful your Angels and Guides may be they cannot step into your body or your mind and live life on your behalf.

Life is a constant source of wonder and yet often you do not notice what is constantly going on around and within you. The very fact that your heart is beating, the sun is shining and the world is turning is a miracle. The whole Universe is a miracle;

you just need to prise open those eyes that are connected to your heart! The design and construction of a building is a miracle, the veins in one small leaf are a miracle, the daily flow of human traffic around the globe is a miracle. Flight, emotion, art, these things are all miracles and yet it is possible to look at a tree, or a leaf, or a wave breaking on the beach and not really see it at all.

Please don't put your ability to appreciate life on hold until it is time to die; it will be too late for you then. Too late to enjoy the miracles of your friends and family, too late to enjoy the miracle of a delicious meal, too late to thrill to the warmth of a bath or the pleasure of a good laugh. There are many other worlds beyond the one you now inhabit, but none of them are exactly like Earth. Your experience of life here is unique, so I urge you to make the most of it and love it with all your heart. Teach yourself once more to be inspired by all that you have in your extraordinary, beautiful and magnificent everyday lives.

Should you ever run out of things to feel amazed about, all you need do is consider the people in your life. Whether you know them a little or a lot, it is likely that you do not know all that they have been through, overcome, learned, created and achieved. Look at the person walking down the street towards you and, forgetting the fact that you have never met them, allow your heart to go out to them in a friendly way, recognising them as your kin. For I would lay very good odds that they have faced just as many challenges and had just as many triumphs in life as you have, and they too would have a marvellous story to tell.

When we truly absorb the impact and meaning of Kuthumi's wise words it is easy to comprehend why seeing each day as new and full of possibility is essential to feeling inspired. Nothing limits your potential to live an inspired and fulfilling life more than imagining you already know what is going to happen. The truth is we have no idea what is possible and what could happen in any moment.

Some people might find this idea unsettling because they are worried that something 'bad' might happen. Bad, unpleasant and undesirable things happen all the time and not once has living your life with blinkers on been able to prevent that. Numbing ourselves and pretending that we don't notice is no way to create an inspiring life. If you view your life as predictable, tell yourself that you already need to know all that is worthwhile about the people in your life, or if you see yourself as being on a treadmill then it is time to take Monsieur Proust's advice and choose to see your world with new eyes.

The first casualty of this kind of thinking is curiosity. The second casualty is usually your willingness to accept that there is more to everything in your life including the people you work with, your neighbours, your job, your partner or spouse, your children and your friends. Your veiled eyes sum everything and everyone up in an instant, labelling them one way or another so that you can slot them into a category you feel safe with. One of the classic ways that this shows up in my line of work is when a client or student admits to keeping their interest in the spiritual and metaphysical to themselves. 'Oh my spouse/partner/colleagues/boss/friends/parents/siblings wouldn't understand. They would probably just laugh at me if they knew I was reading this book or if I told them I have Angels and that I talk with my Intuitive Mind. They just wouldn't get it.'

So I challenge people who say they believe these kinds of ideas to share their interest or experiences with a couple of people in their lives, just to see what happens. They *always* come back flushed with excitement and full of stories about the positive reactions they encountered. Numerous clients and students have found that their friends and colleagues have also been privately interested in the same things, sometimes for years, but never knew who to talk to about it. Some of my students now have an absolute ball giving other people in the office a chakra balance during their lunch break! It is amazing what happens when you give people the credit for being capable of more than you expect and look at them with new eyes.

Imagine, just for a moment, that there is so much more available to you in life than your conscious mind can conceive of or grasp. Why would you want to put limits on your own potential and what you could do with your life? Stop pretending that you know what is going to happen and start being more present, spontaneous and open. In a Universe where stars explode and are reformed, animals communicate with sonar waves, every snow flake is an individual design and no two human beings are ever exactly alike, why is it that we have made ourselves so small? Why is it that we chain ourselves to the notion that we are born to go to school, get a job, have kids, work to pay off the mortgage, retire, get old and ill and then die? Our bland, production-line view of how we are supposed to live life has all but blinded us to the miracles that are happening every day.

Personally, I find it difficult to accept the idea of boredom. I believe that boredom is something we use as an excuse to stop us from trying new things or making the necessary changes we need in our lives. If you are bored with something in your life you are either viewing it in a superficial way, not exercising your curiosity or are using it as something to hide behind. The solution is to go out of your way to get to know that person better, or appreciate what is positive about that situation. Motivate yourself to see the small daily miracles inherent in it, or leave it behind and move on.

It can also be very revealing to take a long look at your expectations and notice how they affect what you get back from life. If you expect your job to be boring and repetitive, the customers to be annoying and the boss to be demanding then that will most likely be your experience. When you are more open minded and are willing to see the best in people, willing to acknowledge that everyone is doing the best they can, that we all need a little help sometimes and that we are all on the steep learning curve called Life, suddenly your life will take on a whole new quality.

You will also find that seeing the best in people also, miraculously, brings out the best in you and that expecting the best from people makes life so much better all round. In this context 'expecting' the best from people does not mean you now have licence to place more demands on everyone. It means you are willing to see what they are truly capable of, give them credit for their abilities and achievements and accept that what you know or assume about them is only a tiny proportion of the fullness of who they truly are. You learn to respect others, even when you don't understand them, and are inspired by everyone because there really is no such thing as an ordinary person.

SEEING YOUR WORLD THROUGH NEW EYES

REQUIREMENTS: Your journal and a pen.

OPTIONAL: Gentle music, candles, incense.
Anything you like to create a pleasant atmosphere.

TIME REQUIRED: 10 to 15 minutes.

HOW OFTEN SHOULD I DO THIS? Anytime you notice yourself feeling uninspired, bored or jaded with any area of your life.

♦ **Journal exercise** – Write a short story about your everyday life and environment, including the people in it, as though you had never seen them or anything in your surroundings before. Describe in detail all the things you notice about your life and the people in it as seen through your new eyes. Let your imagination flow, tune into the colour, vibrancy, uniqueness and even quirkiness of the people and situations you encounter on a regular basis. Write about what is special, valuable and beautiful in your world. A few pages filled with your new observations will be enough to show you that there is a whole *new* world there just waiting for you to see.

- When you have finished writing your miraculous story take a moment to compare this version of your life to how you have perceived it in the past.

- Make a commitment to yourself that you will use your new eyes from now on.

Christopher's Experience

It makes me cringe now, to think back on how blasé I used to be about my life. I took people for granted, believing that I had correctly summed them up and that they had little more to offer. I was bored with my career too and feeling very frustrated with my life. I was very sceptical about doing this exercise and to be honest, I did it to humour my girlfriend, who had insisted I see BelindaGrace in the first place.

Looking back, I guess you could say that I surrendered to the process; tentatively at first and then the story began to flow. I wrote for quite a few pages and found that I was enjoying myself and I began to realise that seeing the world with new eyes could bring something special to my life.

It has taken some time for the people in my office to become accustomed to the 'new me', who asks them how they are feeling or what they did on the weekend and actually listens. I have discovered things about colleagues at work that amaze me even now, but in the past I had written them off as boring. When I go to the beach I make time to appreciate the beauty instead of blocking life with my old 'been there, done that' attitude.

I really believe that the more I reach out and touch life, the more it reaches back to me. I don't know how else to describe it, I feel more connected to everything and everyone around me.

Christopher W.
London, England

CHAPTER ELEVEN

THE POWER OF POSITIVE HABITS

We must be willing to let go of the life we've planned, so as to have the life that is waiting for us. The old skin has to be shed before the new one can come.

JOSEPH CAMPBELL
AUTHOR
1904–1987

It is easy to appreciate that most human beings are creatures of habit. We prefer the familiar to the unknown most of the time, which again goes back to our primal roots, at which time eating an unknown berry or grass, or wandering into unknown terrain, may have proved dangerous or even fatal. Our habitual behaviours make life comforting and give us a sense of being in control; they provide a sense of security. One of the most common examples of turning habitual behaviours into commercial success is the business of franchising. When a product or service is packaged identically everywhere in the world and delivers the same thing no matter where you are, it is reassuring because you know what you are going to get for your effort and money.

Habits also help us to avoid disappointment and deal with the fear of the unknown. They help to maintain structure and order and can have many positive side effects – if, for example, one of your habits is to exercise regularly or to always put a portion of your salary into a savings account. How your habits affect you and your life is very much up to you, especially when it comes to habitual thinking.

If you are prone to regular thoughts that are worrisome, gloomy, negative or critical then choosing to change that style of habitual thinking can vastly improve your life. It seems obvious, I know, but it is so important because your habitual thinking is the lens through which you see yourself, your life and the world. There have been many books over the years that have emphasised the important benefits that arise from positive thinking. You may even have some on your own bookshelf. The point we are making here however is that it needs to become a habit. It is just as easy to turn a behaviour that serves you into a habit as it is to create one that doesn't, so why not make the most of this tool?

One of the habits I would like to encourage you to get into is the habit of thinking and saying 'yes!' to life more often, instead of 'no'. I frequently notice that when a new idea, way of doing things or attitude is suggested, most people will be all too happy to give you a million reasons why it will never happen, why they are fine as they are and don't need to consider other possibilities or why it can't be done. Your willingness to be open to new ideas, products, services, attitudes and ways of doing things could be the difference between a fulfilling life or not. Unless you are deliriously happy with all aspects of your life there may well be room for a different set of habits.

A simple and effective approach to shifting your current vibration is to have a look at your routine and where it is possible to alter it in small ways at first. We often have habits and routines for no particular reason at all. 'It's how I have always done it', most people would say. But in order to make yourself available to a realm of new and exciting possibilities in life it may be beneficial to refresh the ways you go about your everyday routine. Why not try walking a different way to the bus stop in the morning, sitting in a different carriage on the train, having something completely different for lunch, wearing your hair differently, going for a walk early in the morning instead of after work, listening to a different radio station – just to name a few ideas. You have nothing to lose and, as they say, a change is as good as a holiday!

The following exercise will help you to focus and become much more aware of the negative thoughts that churn through your mind and allow you to start to replace them with more inspiring and uplifting ones. All it really takes is repetition, and there is a very good reason for that. On a physical level the brain develops neural pathways for every thought and action we repeatedly use or perform.

A neural pathway is literally a chain or channel of neurons in the brain that are the human equivalent of hard wiring. That is how many actions become automatic with practice, like driving a manual car. You don't have to think about changing gears after a while because the pathways for that action have been physically created in your brain. This hard wiring takes a while to change, but it does change. So, for instance, if you had to change from a gear stick on the floor of the car to one on the steering column, it would feel awkward for a while, and then eventually would become second nature as your brain rewires itself. Now you are going to do a little of your own rewiring, using this simple exercise.

DEVELOPING POSITIVE HABITS

REQUIREMENTS: Your journal and a pen.

OPTIONAL: Go and sit somewhere you have never sat before when writing in your journal.

TIME REQUIRED: 5 minutes.

HOW OFTEN SHOULD I DO THIS? Every day.

◆ **Journal exercise** – Write down all the positive ways of thinking and believing you would like to turn into a habit, then choose a different one each week and write this positive belief in your journal 20 times each day. After seven days, choose another positive thought or belief from your list and write that in your journal twenty times a day, until you have worked your way through the whole list.

Hanna's Experience

This simple habit-changing exercise has helped me in some very interesting ways. First of all I would never have considered myself to be a negative thinker, so my initial realisation that I did actually have a lot of negative thoughts swirling around in my mind was a wake up call in itself.

Then, when I wrote the list of positive thoughts and beliefs in my journal, I could feel something very personal and emotional opening up inside me. Dreams and ideals that I thought had died away were resurrected and they stirred my Soul. I was diligent with this exercise – I still am. It connects me with my inner truth in a direct and simple way. The words I write in my journal are now uppermost in my mind as I go about my day. Rather than thinking about what is wrong with me or the world like I used to, I now think about the many blessings in my life and the ideals that are so important to me.

Hanna T.
Melbourne, Australia

CHAPTER TWELVE

RAISING YOUR VIBRATION – UPGRADING YOUR ENERGY GRIDLINES

In the years that I have been coming to BelindaGrace for readings so many empowering things have happened, but upgrading my energy gridlines is my favourite. Each time I feel so different; lighter, stronger and clearer in every way. Thanks for teaching me this technique, I love being able to do the upgrades for myself, it's so exciting!

ELLEN K.
SYDNEY, AUSTRALIA

There is a saying that you are sure to be familiar with – 'like attracts like' – and when it comes to your own personal frequency or vibration truer words have never been spoken. Think of someone you know who often has a negative or aggressive 'vibe' about them, or how your day can go rapidly down hill after one small thing puts you in a bad mood. Then cast your mind to a person that you know who is generally positive, upbeat and nice to be around, or to the times in your life when you felt happy and in the flow. Can you see how in each of those scenarios the energy or vibration that you or the other person were emanating had an influence on what they experienced from the outside world?

Raising your own vibration is a powerful way to lift your overall sense of well being, open you to a greater connection with your Divine Guidance and have a positive effect on the circumstances of your life. Everything in the Universe gives off a certain frequency and today you are going to learn how to take yours up to the next level.

It has been many years now since my Angels and Spirit Guides taught me about the Energy Gridlines and how to upgrade them for my clients and myself, and the whole process never ceases to impress and amaze me. In truth, it is not actually me who does anything; I play the role of the observer who describes the whole process to my client as it happens.

The Energy Gridlines (EGs) are a network of horizontal and vertical beams of energy and Light that pass through and around your body forming a three-dimensional grid or mesh. They are part of our spiritual anatomy and help to create a form and structure from which our physical body will also benefit. They look a bit like those three-dimensional grids you see in computerised illustrations of a human being, mapping across and up and down our entire form and creating a network all around us.

Everybody has these EGs, and from time to time they need to be upgraded. When the existing gridlines that are currently in and around you become depleted they can be removed and replaced with a beautiful, brand new set. Think of an old fluorescent light tube that is running out of steam, its light becomes dull and starts to flicker. When you take it out and put a new one in, the whole room is brightened up again.

Each EG gives off a vibration or frequency that forms part of the overall 'vibe' that you exude and is also a reflection of the level of consciousness you are currently at. Each set of EGs will be a certain colour – so for instance the EGs in and around you now may be red and the new set that will replace them may be blue or green. There is no hierarchy in the sequence of colours your EGs take. You may upgrade from red to blue, while someone else may upgrade from blue to red. There is no competition or scale by which to measure yourself against others; there is no colour that is best or better than another; it is your own individual progression that matters. As far as I can tell, there is no limit to the number of upgrades you can have during the course of a lifetime, because there is actually no limit to the levels of awareness that we can achieve.

Having said that though, my Angels and Spirit Guides advise that on average, most people who are consciously pursuing their spiritual path in some way (that means you!) will be due for an EGs upgrade approximately once a year. This is quite a new thing for me and I feel it is very exciting. In the past the EGs upgrade has happened for me and my clients at unpredictable intervals, sometimes with a gap of several years in between. Now we are being shown that our journeys of evolution and higher awareness are speeding up and can progress in a more methodical and deliberate way. I believe that this new information is so significant because a growing number of people are eager to be on their spiritual path and to connect with that all important level of life and themselves.

To be given the green light to proceed with our EGs upgrades on a regular basis, rather than just wait until they happen, is like a vote of confidence in those of us who do want to raise our own vibration and that of the whole human race. It only takes one candle to create Light for many others. So now we can all become brighter candles with our flames shining more clearly through the night. Spirit knows that we want to get on track and are willing to do what is necessary. The EGs upgrade is a gift, a reward and the equivalent of a spiritual graduation ceremony.

A new set of EGs not only signifies a shift in the level of your consciousness, it can actually help you to attain the improved levels you desire. It's a cycle really, so who can say with 100% certainty which comes first? The key is to follow the process I am about to describe now and once a year from now on, or when you feel that you have just had or are on the verge of a breakthrough in your life. That way you can view the new set of EGs as a reward for what you have just accomplished or a way of helping you to get there. It is important to be honest with yourself about where you are at. The EGs are not toys to be played around with, they are very important components of your spiritual anatomy, so if you should attempt to give yourself an EGs upgrade and the timing isn't right, your Angels and Guides will look after you and make sure it doesn't happen. When the time is right, however, they will actually do it for you and all you need to do is relax and observe. In that sense, then, this 'exercise' isn't really about you 'doing' anything; it's about witnessing a beautiful process that will help you live an inspired and purposeful life.

UPGRADING YOUR ENERGY GRIDLINES

REQUIREMENTS: A place to lay down comfortably and relax without interruption.
Your journal and a pen.

OPTIONAL: Some soft quiet music, a candle, incense etc. to help you create a soothing atmosphere.

TIME REQUIRED: around 20 minutes.

How often should I do it? A minimum of once a year or whenever you feel you have just had a positive shift in your consciousness or awareness – an 'ah-ha moment'.

Or, whenever you feel that you have been working diligently towards a positive shift in your consciousness or awareness and need that last little push to help you along.

◆ Once you have set your room up the way you would like it, lie down and get comfortable. It is preferable to stay awake and aware through the whole process so don't make the room too dark or cover yourself in lots of heavy blankets. Just be comfortable enough to relax.

- Remind yourself that your intention is to have an Energy Gridline upgrade and that you are ready to witness the upgrade taking place if the time is right.

- Ask all of your Angels and Spirit Guides to come and gather around you and request that they facilitate an Energy Gridline upgrade for you. You may wish to let them know why it is that you feel it is time for an upgrade. Sometimes you will feel that you have earned it and other times you may feel that you need an upgrade to help you make that final leap to the next level of your awareness. Either way, talking to them about it will help you to feel even clearer about why you feel your personal vibration is lifting. Or if it is your annual time just relax and say "here I am!"

Note: your Angels and Spirit Guides will not be judging you or assessing you at this time. It is not a matter of being 'good enough' or 'deserving it'. The Universe and your Angels and Guides are very fair and objective in this way. If it's the right time for an upgrade you will get one and if it's not the right time you won't. That's just the way it is, not a comment on you as a person. The more attuned you become to your inner world and spiritual path the more accurate you will become at gauging whether it's time for an Energy Gridline upgrade or not. The most important thing is to make yourself available for an upgrade whenever you feel it may be possible or necessary.

- Close your eyes and try to picture your current set of EGs. You may get a sense of the lines of energy and Light flowing across and up and down through your body, sometimes through a gentle humming or buzzing feeling, sometimes by seeing them or getting a sense of their existing colour. Just go with the first impressions that come to you.

◆ Imagine that you can step outside your body and look at yourself. Can you see yourself lying there and the gridlines criss-crossing through you? Use whatever visualisation approach works best for you and stay gently focused on whatever information you are given.

◆ There is often a brief period of waiting patiently before the actual removal of the EGs begins. Keep breathing deeply and steadily, reminding yourself that your Angels and Guides are going to do the work for you and all you need to do is stay awake. It's a bit like going to have a massage. You don't need to tell the masseuse what to do every step of the way and you will enjoy it more if you simply let go, make yourself available and allow the expert to do their work.

◆ At some point you will feel the old gridlines being removed. Certain areas of your body may tingle slightly, or even relax more in an area where you didn't even realise you were holding tension. Your tummy might gurgle or you may begin to yawn. Some people, myself included, even get a sensation of the beams actually being drawn out. It is a lovely sensation, like a caress or a gentle tickle, with the added bonus of the knowledge that something old is being removed so it can be replaced by something brighter and fresher.

Note: It is not essential to feel or even see the removal process. It's nice if you can but it doesn't impede the process if you can't. Your role is one of willingness and lying still for long enough to allow your Angels and Guides to do the work. Because my clairvoyant sight is so developed I can easily see my team working around me, which is wonderful of course, but in the early days of working with this process I usually only perceived the colours of the EGs and sometimes a pair or two of hands pulling the old ones out and putting the new ones in.

◆ For those of you have worked to develop your clairvoyant sight, you may have the pleasure of watching some of your own team removing your old EGs. Notice how gracefully and efficiently they go about their task. Rather than fretting about whether or not you are 'doing it properly', relax and enjoy the treat. Sometimes they will remove the EGs from head to toe, at other times from side to side first, and so on. The order in which they are removed doesn't matter, so just go with the flow.

◆ The next step is certainly my favourite part and something very special. When all your old EGs have been removed there will be a pause of a few seconds before your team begin to put the new EGs in place. In my clairvoyant sight those few seconds show the human

energy field to be this vast place, like outer space –
endless and peaceful. It is the pause between the out-
breath and the next inhalation. It can be a moment of
pure bliss where you can be completely still.

◆ Then your team will begin putting in the new EGs.
Perhaps you can discern their colour or you can ask your
Angels and Guides to tell you what colour your new set
is. The placing of the new set is usually quite quick –
about half the time it took to remove the old ones. But
that is just my experience. There are no hard and fast
rules, so trust in what you are experiencing and give your
team enough time to complete the job.

◆ When all your new EGs are in place your Angels and
Guides will then surround you in a lovely cocoon
of shimmering energy and Light – usually white or
pearlescent – but any colour that comes to you is fine.
Lie still for one more minute and take note of how you
feel. Most people report a pleasant, subtle high and feel
replenished and refreshed.

◆ In your journal, make a note of the date, the colour of
the EGs that were removed and the colour of your new
Energy Gridlines. Note down anything else that you wish
to about your experience, as it will serve as a helpful and
fascinating reminder for you in a year's time. The first time
is always the most difficult because there is so much to
take in when it is all new to you. Making some notes each

time you do an upgrade is a wonderful way of making it easier for you next time.

◆ Congratulations! You have just received an Energy Gridline upgrade.

Over the years, through my own upgrades and what my clients and students have reported to me, the uplifting feeling of the new vibration is noticeable for the next two or three days. After that period of time you begin to become accustomed to your new frequency and it feels normal. This is not the same as the high wearing off. The positive effect of the new EGs will stay with you; what has happened is that you have adjusted to your new frequency and that has become your new operating level. You have made the transition to a new level of awareness.

It is at this point that I would like to make one final suggestion. Now that you have raised your own level of vibration, it is a good idea to make sure that your environment reflects that. Surround yourself with inspiring and uplifting things; tune in to what you are intuitively drawn to rather than sticking with old habits. You may need to change a picture on your wall, buy some beautiful music or make sure you have a fresh bunch of flowers in your home. Make sure you surround yourself with positive people too, so that you can share your bright flame freely with others.

Elizabeth's Experience

Many changes had been occurring in my life and I was feeling quite excited. I had been persevering with my spiritual and personal development and was starting to see some wonderful results. I felt better, but although I couldn't put my finger on it, I also felt like something was still holding me back.

The following day I was tidying up my desk and came across the notes from a course I had done with BelindaGrace the previous year. It had been a while since I had read them and flicking through the pages brought back happy memories of what we had learned. The notes on upgrading Energy Gridlines jumped out at me, so I lay down, called upon my Angels and Spirit Guides to help me and created an intention to do an upgrade for myself.

I felt, rather than saw that my existing gridlines were blue and as BelindaGrace suggests I just trusted that my Angels and Guides would do the work for me. For ten minutes or so I lay there, relaxed and attentive, wondering how I would know when I was 'done'. Next thing I know I felt a lovely tingle pass through my body and I had a clear sense that the process was complete. I wondered to myself what colour the new Gridlines were and saw a flash of bright pink before my eyes. That's good enough for me, I thought!

It wasn't long before the Universe confirmed to me that I had moved into a new vibration. Months earlier I had nervously applied for a place in a music course and had almost been relieved when told that it was full; but when I checked my emails that day I found that a second course had been opened up due to demand and it was even at a time that suited me better.

Since upgrading my Energy Gridlines other pleasant experiences and positive opportunities have come my way that I would not have had the confidence to embrace in the past. I am truly delighted with these results.

ELIZABETH A.
PERTH, AUSTRALIA

CHAPTER THIRTEEN

MEANING, PURPOSE AND FEELING HAPPY

There are two things to aim at in life: first, to get what you want; and after that, to enjoy it. Only the wisest of mankind achieve the second.

LOGAN PEARSALL SMITH
ESSAYIST AND HISTORIAN
1865–1946

Most people are looking for ways to create a sense of meaning and purpose in their lives. What often tends to surprise them is that even the most meaningful events or experiences can have a fleeting effect or lose their gloss over time. This in turn can lead to feelings of disappointment or the belief that there is something else they should be doing. Very little is said in our culture about the nature of happiness itself and its role in securing an ongoing sense of meaning and purpose in life.

My Angels and Spirit Guides inform me that happiness is usually a combination of a number of factors and that it is a quality that anyone can develop from within themselves. They also emphasise that happiness *is* the actual meaning and purpose of our lives. It is, in fact, why we are here. So you could say that learning to be happy within yourself is the purpose of your life and, in turn, will give your life the meaning you desire. To begin with, this way of looking at the role of happiness in our lives is quite confusing because it seems contrary to everything we consider to be normal and real.

The western mind in particular is always looking for the most complicated and difficult kind of approach. There is a deeply rooted belief in our society that nothing worthwhile should be attained without a struggle and that you have to suffer in order to earn the right to be happy. It might seem bizarre at first to realise that you can choose to be happy and keep choosing that perspective throughout your life.

We are also taught to believe that a sense of meaning and purpose in life can only come to you once you have done something notable or found that special thing you are supposed to do or person you are supposed to be with. Sometimes a sense of purpose in life can come from a certain activity or vocation, but we must learn to give meaning to our lives and be happy with or without them. Everything in life is transitory and impermanent. Children eventually grow up and move out of home, entire industries become obsolete and people need to retrain and move on, happy marriages end in old age, and all material possessions eventually wear out.

If your entire sense of purpose revolves around your job, family, creative ability or marriage you immediately put yourself in an uncomfortable position, because your monkey mind will usually cause you some anxiety around it. Some people are even afraid of having too much happiness because the idea of losing it frightens them. So creating a sense of meaning and purpose that comes from within you and is not so subject to external factors is very important. With practice you can come to realise that feeling happy is actually a choice and has more to do with what you decide to fix your thoughts and attention on, than with what is going on around you.

The other thing that I notice repeatedly in my work is the way that many of us keep expecting meaning and purpose to show up, waving a bright banner and saying

'Yoo-hoo, I'm over here!' Very rarely, as far as I can tell, does it ever happen like that. Years ago, when I was very young I had ideas of writing books one day and of being a psychologist. I had no idea that I would find myself being a Clairvoyant Healer, let alone writing books on the topic. Instead, I groped around in the dark for some years, just like everyone else, until I learned to follow the clues that were right in front of me. Which brings me to another point – having a sense of meaning and purpose in life is a journey, not a destination, because you know what? No sooner had I written and published my first book, I started to wonder what my *next* book would be about.

It is always important to remember that it is the simple things in life that can bring us the greatest feelings of contentment. In our headlong rush to find ways to feel inspired about life, the simple things are often overlooked. Many things can bring happiness, meaning and purpose into your life every day, so it pays to focus on them. If something or someone is in your life regularly then it is most likely present because you want it to be or because it is trying to guide you in some way. Other, more ordinary aspects of everyday life can also bring you joy – your pet, a bunch of flowers, a full fruit bowl, a walk in the park, a favourite song… none of these things are headline news, but if they add to your feelings of happiness, then good for you. Don't ever feel like you have to justify them.

CREATING MEANING, PURPOSE AND HAPPINESS IN YOUR LIFE

REQUIREMENTS: Your journal and a pen. Peace and quiet.

OPTIONAL: Soft music, a candle, incense. Anything you like to create a pleasant atmosphere.

TIME REQUIRED: 10 to 15 minutes.

HOW OFTEN SHOULD I DO THIS? At least once.
This can be a great exercise to do on an anniversary of some kind like your Birthday or New Year's Eve.

◆ **Journal exercise** – Write down the things that have given your life meaning and purpose in the past and what gives your life meaning and purpose now. Be sure to note down the entire range of people, activities, experiences and possessions. Don't edit your list based on what you believe other people might think. This is your own private 'Meaning, Purpose and Happiness' list!

◆ Review and add to your list any time you want to feel inspired.

◆ Complete one action – no matter how small – that will help you connect with or develop that source of inspiration in your life; such as searching the internet for eco-holiday destinations, re-reading a book that you found uplifting, making contact with a person who had a positive effect on your life and letting them know how much you appreciate them.

Mitchell's Experience

The way Mitchell's life has panned out so far is a good example of someone who learned how to choose happiness over stagnation and discontent.

In my 20s and 30s I worked extremely hard running my own small business. I worked very long hours and endured considerable stress, but got a genuine buzz out of doing well, using my creativity and spending my money on the cars and motorbikes, boats and outdoor activities that I so loved.

All my life I had always felt a great love for animals, but my hectic lifestyle was not conducive to owning a pet. Not only did I work hard and take part in a lot of sports and hobbies, I also enjoyed travelling and would regularly fly overseas to visit friends and family. Then, a few years ago the industry in which I had been so successful began to change dramatically. Suddenly work slowed down and a number of my closest friends married, had children and no longer had as much time for the cars, bikes and weekends at the soccer ground as I did.

I felt deflated and confused, wondering where I had gone wrong. Then, when scouting around on the internet for ideas for my next holiday, I happened upon a sanctuary for wild bears in Cambodia that rescues these beautiful animals from the cooking pots of local restaurants. I had always wanted to travel to Asia and here was a great reason to go there. Volunteering at the sanctuary for two weeks offered me the security of an organised destination, accommodation, an opportunity to meet and work with other people of like mind and the chance of a lifetime in working with this threatened species of bear.

Not only did I find the whole experience fulfilling and rewarding, I had a lot of fun, made new friends and was able to shift my focus from fretting about my slowing business and changing circumstances. Surprisingly I received offers of work from the people who ran the sanctuary. It turns out that they had been looking for someone with my skills for months. I now go there once a year for a whole month, to volunteer at the sanctuary and take part in fund raising activities both there and at home.

'One of the other things I find so uplifting about spending time in Cambodia is the fact that the people are so friendly, generous and happy. They have so little compared to what we consider to be normal back home. Being there puts my life and concerns into a much healthier perspective. I come back feeling like I have done something useful, made the most of my time, and with a greater appreciation of how wonderful my own life is.'

MITCHELL W.
SYDNEY, AUSTRALIA

All his great experiences unfolded spontaneously because he gradually became more willing to flow with what life was presenting him. He freely admits that he would not have wound his business down to its current level of his own accord and that he had never really foreseen himself living as he does now. When his business first started to dwindle Mitchell was upset and fearful, he fought hard against these changes and even became angry about the cards life was dealing him. He also admits that he found it very difficult to leave his comfort zone and the first two trips to Cambodia were very challenging for him.

Seeing himself predominantly as someone who liked his comfort zones and who didn't deal all that well with change Mitchell learned that despite any effort or will on his part there was a force bigger than himself ringing these changes in his life. Step by step he developed the confidence to choose in the moment, to try something he hoped would bring him some joy and satisfaction, and as a consequence he has been able to discover and develop many forms of meaning and purpose in his life. As Mitchell himself told me;

"Paying your own way to a foreign country in order to sweep out cages and sleep on a grass bed may not be everyone's idea of fun, but I love it and should it ever lose its allure for me I know now that I have the ability and courage to choose again in the future. My other great interest these days is photography and there have been ample opportunities to take some lovely photos at the sanctuary, so who knows where that might lead? The

point is, though, that I don't see meaning and purpose as something that should come to me or that other people must give me. Life is a constant experiment; you never know what is going to bring you that feeling of satisfaction until you try."

CHAPTER FOURTEEN

CONNECTING WITH YOUR INSPIRED SELF

You see things; and you say, 'Why?' But I dream things that never were; and I say, 'Why not?'

GEORGE BERNARD SHAW
PLAYWRIGHT AND WINNER OF
THE NOBEL PRIZE FOR LITERATURE
1856–1950

When it comes to the self-improvement process and the desire you feel to become a better person, it is very important to remind yourself that you already embody all the excellent qualities that you aspire to. The fact that you are touched by the inspiring stories of other people, moved to help others during difficult times and make the effort to have a greater understanding of yourself, means that the qualities of inspiration, compassion, generosity and enlightenment already stir deep within you. If you did not already have an affinity with these ideals to some degree you would not be attracted to them.

In this chapter you will be shown how to bring these innate qualities of yours back into full awareness by connecting with one of your Positive Personality Aspects, known as your Inspired Self. We all have many aspects or facets to our characters, and it is important to spend time focusing on what is beautiful and great about you.

Those of you who are familiar with my previous book, *You are Clairvoyant – Developing the Secret Skill We All Have*, may remember the exercise that helps you to transform the negative aspects of personality we all experience from time to time into their positive counterparts. If you feel that you do have some habitual behaviours that are problematic then you may wish to revisit that exercise some time soon. However this exercise is designed to connect you directly with the Positive Personality Aspect we call your Inspired Self and can be a very uplifting experience.

Goodness, kindness, empathy, compassion, the ability to live an inspired life or any other positive qualities are not like software programs that you can buy and load into your system. They are natural and inherent, and like a seed that has lain dormant for decades or a seedling that hasn't had much room to grow, they only need a little bit of nurturing to bring them fully to life.

EXERCISE TWELVE

CONNECTING WITH YOUR INSPIRED SELF

REQUIREMENTS: Your journal and a pen. Peace and quiet.

OPTIONAL: Gentle music, a candle, incense.
Anything you like to create a pleasant atmosphere.

TIME REQUIRED: 10 to 15 minutes.

HOW OFTEN SHOULD I DO THIS? Whenever you would like to connect with one of your Positive Personality Aspects.

Note: In this process it is very important to let your imagination flow and give it free rein, as it will be translating your Positive Personality Aspect into images and words for you to experience. The whole basis of this process is observation; meaning that when you relax, close your eyes and focus you will be able to observe one of your Positive Personality Aspects as though you were watching it on a movie screen. It is very important for you to understand that it is the simple act of observing this part of yourself that will allow it to become a much more active part of your conscious awareness again. This will be the process that makes it possible for you to acknowledge all that is good and natural within yourself – your essential and highest truth.

The act of observing and paying attention to it means that it is no longer hidden or ignored; seeing, and in this case, sensing, is believing. Allow yourself to feel the full impact of its positive vibration and beauty. You don't have to do anything other than observe – meaning that you listen to, watch and feel this part of you as it expresses itself without hindrance.

Please don't become concerned about whether or not you are going to 'see' anything at first, that will come with practice, and there will be plenty of opportunities to practise as you have many different Positive Personality Aspects to observe. Observing means to have a sense of, to be aware of and to feel; it is designed to be a gentle process so that you can enjoy the full impact of all that is positive about you.

◆ Sit or lie down somewhere that you feel comfortable and relaxed. Focus your intention on the fact that you are going to connect with and observe your Inspired Self. This is the Positive Aspect of your personality that feels inspired and moved by life and by people and which genuinely wants to live an inspired and inspiring life.

◆ Relax and imagine that you are going to meet a new friend who will show up like an image in your mind, a feeling or a presence or even as a voice who will speak to you. All you have to do is give it your attention, just remain relaxed and open-minded. On your first attempt it may take a few minutes before you get a sense of anything. Don't be impatient; these parts of your personality are accustomed to staying in the background, usually until they are called upon by extraordinary circumstances. Give your Inspired Self a chance to adjust to the idea that you are now ready to embrace and reunite it.

◆ Gradually you will get a sense of a figure or character emerging. If your clairvoyant sight isn't very clear yet it can be more like a feeling that someone has arrived; a bit like when you know that someone has come into the room without even having to look around; you simply feel their presence. Whatever you see, hear or feel will be good enough. The most important part of this process is to keep reminding yourself that this uplifting and positive energy comes from within you. What you are doing consciously is simply being the witness, that is your role; and by being the willing observer you automatically create a space for the deeper connection to occur.

◆ Staying as relaxed and focused as you can, continuing to breathe deeply, let your aspect express itself in any way it likes; your imagination will find some amazing ways to translate the energy of your Inspired Self and its qualities to you. Enjoy your observation time, look for all the detail you can, tune into how you are feeling within yourself and continue to listen attentively, as though someone is about to say something very important, and just let the information come.

◆ In this process you are rebuilding the bridges between your conscious mind and all the positive belief and knowing that is inherent in your nature. Allow yourself to *feel and know* it in your body, heart and solar plexus.

◆ Eventually you will notice yourself losing focus or your Inspired Aspect will start to fade away. This is a good time to finish your contact for today. In your mind or out loud, tell your Inspired Self in your own words how you feel about the experience you have just had. Thank your Inspired Self for revealing itself and let it know that you would like to have more contact soon.

◆ When you are ready, open your eyes and write in your journal everything you can remember about your Inspired Self and your thoughts, realisations and feelings throughout the process. Every time you connect, the quality of the experience will improve and you will perceive new things, so it is a great idea to have your journal handy each time.

◆ Over time, you will find that there are many Positive Personality Aspects you can become reacquainted with. Your own personal list may include such aspects as Compassion, Forgiveness, Abundance, Vitality, Generosity, Happiness, Clairvoyance, Intuitiveness, Empowerment, Optimism, Manifestation, Confidence, Kindness and so on. Don't limit yourself! Keep asking every time you go in to connect with your Inspired Self – What other Positive Personality Aspects do I have?

Please reunite me with more. I have no doubt you will be pleasantly surprised more than once!

It is very important that we begin the journey of discovering what is great and wonderful about ourselves. This is just as much a part of the healing and self-awareness process as becoming aware of characteristics that do not serve us. Now is the time to stop regarding yourself as someone who needs to be fixed in some way and start seeing yourself as a multi-faceted jewel that is now being fully revealed. Ultimately the ideal way of being is to strive for balance on a daily basis. A truly balanced person accepts and understands that he or she is not perfect, but that they do have all the qualities within themselves to help them resolve any behaviour or belief that they should choose to transform. Now is the time when we can all take the opportunity to transform our vision of ourselves as troubled beings to a people who are committed to reconnecting with and acting upon the answers.

ANGELA'S EXPERIENCE

I grew up believing that there was something wrong with me; not much about me that was worthwhile. My mother was an alcoholic and my father coped with that by staying away from home as much as possible. I kept quiet and stayed out of their way to avoid getting into trouble; especially from my mother who would fly off the handle at the slightest provocation.

Mostly I was told how stupid I was and made to feel that I was a nuisance. I used to wonder why my parents ever bothered having children.

I did a lot of conventional therapy before starting to explore my spiritual life. I found hope in that approach after years of slow analysis. When my Angels and Spirit Guides first introduced me to my Inspired Self and told me that I had Positive Personality Aspects I was dumbfounded; I couldn't believe that there was anything worthwhile inside me.

Connecting with my Inspired Self has helped me to turn my life around. I don't just go through the motions of life anymore; I am actually living – really feeling alive. I get excited about things, make plans and set goals. In the space of one year I have gone from having a life that seemed to have no meaning to having some sense of purpose, things to look forward to and a positive view of myself. I know that there is more clearing still to be done, but if I get a little down or disillusioned, as we all do sometimes, I think about my Inspired Self and her energy lifts me back up.

ANGELA J.
LONDON, ENGLAND

CHAPTER FIFTEEN

CALMING YOUR MONKEY MIND

The soul loves to meditate, for in contact with the Spirit lies its greatest joy. If then you experience mental resistance during meditation, remember that reluctance to meditate comes from the ego; it does not belong to the soul.

PARAMAHANSA YOGANANDA
AUTHOR OF *AUTOBIOGRAPHY OF A YOGI*
SPIRITUAL LEADER AND FOUNDER OF
THE SELF REALISATION FELLOWSHIP
1893–1952

One of the easiest ways to connect more freely with your natural intuitive and clairvoyant abilities is to gradually tame and calm your Monkey Mind. The Monkey Mind has been described in various ways over the centuries, often, as Yogananda says, as the ego or ego-based mind. The term Monkey Mind is one that my Angels and Guides like to use as a way of indicating that it is not a bad thing, but like a playful, demanding, noisy and self centred creature it requires some discipline to bring the best out in it.

Your Monkey Mind is the level of your mind that is always analysing, worrying, questioning yourself, doubting, scheming, falling prey to fears, gossiping, criticising and so on; its chatter is loud and ceaseless. It is not a separate compartment in your head, but it tends to act that way and can pull you off course, causing you to doubt the clear messages your intuition sends you and to resist many good things that the Universe brings into your life. Your Monkey Mind will always calculate, compete and compare. In its world nothing is ever easy or natural, there is always a price, an obligation or a condition. This level of your mind is attached to everything. It believes it owns this, wants that and that there is never enough to go around. It creates a 'lack' mentality and causes you unhealthy stress; yet taming this unruly little creature is easily within your grasp.

There are a number of simple ways to do this, such as the earlier exercise of developing more positive habits, especially positive thoughts. But no matter how hard we try we cannot escape the fact that the most effective way to calm the Monkey Mind is through meditation; something which most people I meet claim to have tried and feel they weren't very 'good' at. There are many styles of meditation and many ways to meditate, so after some experimentation everyone can find a method that suits them. Finding a way that is effective for you is very important for your personal growth and your capacity to live an inspired and meaningful life.

Meditation is so beneficial because it creates a time and space for you to get back in touch with your body and your feelings, which is where the clues to your inspiration reside. It helps you get out of your busy head space, that is usually dominated by activity, timetables and worries. So a calm mind also equals freedom, which is something we all yearn for deep down. Interesting, isn't it? That we often put so much time and effort into our attempts to feel free when sitting quietly with yourself for only a few minutes a day can take you there directly.

It is not my intention here to write a book about the virtues of meditating and in any case, I think you already know or at least suspect what they are. My job is just to keep reminding you how important and beneficial it is so that you won't keep putting it off. It is never a matter of being 'good at' meditating or not. The important thing is that you do it and gradually turn it into another healthy habit; your own best practice will develop with time and patience.

CALMING YOUR MONKEY MIND

REQUIREMENTS: A peaceful location handy to your home or workplace.

OPTIONAL: A cushion, rug or portable seat you can use outdoors.

TIME REQUIRED: 10 to 15 minutes

HOW OFTEN SHOULD I DO THIS? Preferably every day.

◆ Go and sit outside, somewhere comfortable and pleasant, away from your telephones and all other distractions. Sit somewhere comfortable and relax. Then focus on one thing only – a cloud, a tree, the ocean, the grass in front of your feet – and breathe steadily and calmly for 10 minutes. If you notice yourself thinking about something, drop the thought immediately and give your full attention back to your breathing and whatever you are focusing on.

◆ You may close your eyes if you wish and focus on a sensation such as the breeze in your hair, the sun on your face and so on. Remain aware of your breathing and keep it calm and steady, letting go of any thoughts as they arise.

Note: one of the best indications that you are making progress is your increasing ability to drop a thought as soon as you notice it. When I first began meditating I would notice I was thinking about something but was so attached to my thoughts I 'had' to follow the thought, idea or story through to the end before I could let it go. One day, to my surprise, I realised I wasn't doing this anymore and that I was taking my attention back to my breathing without having to finish the sentence I had just become aware of. This may seem like a small step, but when you can do it you will understand how good it feels and the difference between your Monkey Mind running you or not.

◆ After you have sat and focused in this way for ten minutes there is nothing else to do, that's it! Your meditation is complete. Acknowledge yourself, say a blessing or stand and perform the Thanksgiving to Mother Earth, the first exercise in this book then enjoy the rest of your day.

I hope that you come to relish your times of simple meditation, whether you do them outdoors or inside. Even if the weather is inclement you can still find a window to look out of, just be sure to switch off your phone and any other distractions before you begin.

This kind of quiet contemplation has made it possible for me to hone my intuitive and clairvoyant abilities over the years and it will have the same effect for you. If you wish to hear your intuitive messages more clearly a calm mind is essential. While I am meditating I often receive helpful messages from my own Angels or beautiful Beings like Archangel Gabriel. Here are some wise words of encouragement from him to help you persevere with your meditation practice.

Greetings my dear friends; I come to you at this time in order to offer you support. In the past you may have found the prospect and practice of meditation daunting; so accustomed are you to maintaining a high level of activity and output. A great deal of human life focuses on action and in light of that the practice of meditation may seem pointless or even dull. Connecting with the world inside yourself is anything but dull, however, because you are a wondrous Being and ultimately it is only quiet contemplation that can take you fully into your inner world.

You must regard every minute of meditation you are able to accomplish as a worthwhile achievement; just one minute is an important step along your spiritual road. When you are restless in mind and body during these quiet times do not chastise yourself for not practising well. Shower yourself in praise and thanks for the effort you have made and remain gently committed to the task. Consider also that I am by your side, helping you along.

When you sit to meditate do so with an intention to make peace within yourself and in your mind, offering yourself therefore as a vessel for the harmonious Universal energy of Love.

Heather's Experience

I am so glad BelindaGrace shared this method with me, I find it a much easier way to meditate and calm my busy mind. I have always been an active person who loves being outside, but I feel the real key is that I leave my home and office behind and free myself of all that mental and emotional clutter for a while.

Recently I went and sat under a lovely old fig tree in a park near my home and began to contemplate the elegant branch that curved down in front of me. As my tension and revolving thoughts began to fade away a large white feather drifted down through the leaves and landed in my lap! I was so thrilled and felt that my Angels were saying hello to me.

Giving myself permission to have ten minutes completely to myself and connecting to the wonderful energy of Nature has made calming my Monkey Mind an experience I look forward to each day.

Heather Z.
Adelaide, Australia

CHAPTER SIXTEEN

WANT WHAT YOU HAVE, THEN YOU WILL ALWAYS HAVE WHAT YOU WANT

The secret of health for both mind and body is not to mourn for the past, worry about the future, or anticipate troubles, but to live in the present moment wisely and earnestly.

BUDDHA
560–480 BC

It may seem ironic to some, but accepting rather than just tolerating the things you already have in your life is the first step to changing or letting go of what you aren't too thrilled about. Remember that old saying 'what you resist persists'? Well, this is the opposite of resistance. It is an unravelling process that will help you to understand how certain things in your life have evolved and the ramifications of some of your choices. It can also help you to see the silver linings in the clouds and appreciate what you have learned along the way.

In this context 'wanting' what you have actually means acknowledging everything rather than pretending what you don't like isn't happening and hoping it will go away of its own accord. (Ac)Knowledge(ing) is power, and this kind of self awareness is priceless. Which brings me to another well known saying – 'the definition of insanity is doing the same thing over and over again and expecting a different result.'

It's time to stop the insanity and retrace some of your steps so that you can discover which approaches worked for you and what might need a bit of revision. Most of us are always in a hurry to get to our next goal or destination in life, causing many people to be more focused on what they hope will happen in the future rather than what is actually going on in the present moment. Before you can effectively set sail for your next port of call you really need to know where you are starting from. Can you imagine calling a taxi company and asking them to drive you to the airport without being able to give them the address they need to pick you up from? You could tell them you need to get to the airport as much as you like, but until you can tell them where you are starting your journey from they would not be able to help you. Any good navigator will tell you that you cannot set a new course without accurate bearings on your current location.

Your Intuitive Mind longs to be your loyal navigator. It is steering you towards wanting what you have first, because it is vital to live in the present moment if you want to live a life of meaning and purpose *and* feel inspired. Wanting what you currently have frees you up to make better choices from now on. As you learn different ways to connect and create with your natural intuition and clairvoyance you are also developing your ability to listen to your Little Voice more on a daily basis and allowing it to guide you. This next exercise will help you to see how you arrived at your current situation and circumstances, and what role using or ignoring your intuition may have played.

HOW DID I GET WHERE I AM?

REQUIREMENTS: Your journal and a pen. Peace and quiet.

OPTIONAL: Gentle music, a candle, incense.
Anything you like to create a pleasant atmosphere.

TIME REQUIRED: 10 to 15 minutes.

HOW OFTEN SHOULD I DO THIS? At least once and then anytime you would like to trace the origins of a certain situation in your life.

◆ **Journal exercise** – Divide your page into two columns. In one column note down some of the things you have in your life that you like and are happy to acknowledge. In the other, write down some of the things you don't like and prefer to ignore. Pick an item from each column and then work backwards in time to uncover the moment in your life when this situation was created.

◆ Take particular notice of the choices you made at each turn that helped to bring the situation into being.

◆ Think back and consider where you responded to your inner knowing and the guidance of your Intuitive Mind and where you ignored, rejected or suppressed it. Can you see how using and responding to your intuition would have improved any of these outcomes? Maybe you even feel that the things you like and want would be better if you had used your intuition more fully.

♦ Contemplate your findings and commit them to memory. Remember, the definition of insanity is doing the same thing over and over and expecting a different result. What have you learned from this exercise? Has it increased the way you value your intuitive nudges and inner wisdom? Promise yourself to take more notice of them from now on.

CHRISTINA'S EXPERIENCE

When I retraced my steps over the last fifteen years I focused mainly on the fact that I have never had a job I really enjoyed. It amazed me when I discovered that I regularly ignored my Intuitive Mind when it tried to guide me towards something better. My Intuitive Mind always told me that I was more talented than my CV revealed. I had left school early and always felt I compared badly to people who had gone on to college or university. Other people would always get promoted ahead of me. I never had any trouble getting the job initially, but I never progressed. Every time my IM would urge me to go and ask for a promotion, more responsibility or even a pay rise, I would always tell it to go away. I truly believed that everyone else had the same low opinion of my skills. So I would get frustrated after a couple of years without a promotion, only to leave and find myself in the same situation somewhere else.

After I did the 'How did I get where I am?' exercise I saw that I was ignoring my inner wisdom. I made an appointment to see the HR manager in my company and told her all. She was so understanding and even told me that people had commented about my good work and manner, adding that my apparent lack of confidence was unwarranted.

She immediately arranged for me to attend a training course and now I am the PA to the sales manager, which is a truly exciting and challenging role. I am so pleased with the changes in my working life and glad that I now have a greater respect for my intuitive guidance.

CHRISTINA J.
PERTH, AUSTRALIA

CHAPTER SEVENTEEN

MANIFESTING YOUR HEART'S DESIRE

Through my Angels and Guides I learned that the body is the spiritual processing plant, which includes the spiritual anatomy such as your chakras and your channel. Your spiritual anatomy and physical anatomy work together as one system. To my delight I have found that when you care for both and bring them into harmony you enhance your spiritual awareness and create the life you desire ...

ADRIAN O.
SYDNEY, AUSTRALIA

Many of us have been brought up to believe that the most effective way to create the kind of life we desire and 'get what we want' is to put in a certain amount of effort and energy. We place a great deal of emphasis on 'doing', which can lead to a lack of balance in our lives and disrupt the interaction between our physical and spiritual anatomy. Our goal now is to utilise all levels of our Being to create an inspiring life by taking a more wholistic approach to manifestation, achievement and fulfilment. We all want the good things in life and a wholistic approach will restore inner harmony and bring you what you need, as well as want, in a more graceful manner.

'Holistic', or 'Wholistic' as it was originally and I believe more properly spelled, is derived from the root word 'whole' and in this case means the 'whole' person. It is the whole of you that is involved in your personal growth and the journey along your spiritual path – your body included. Mystics, yogis and practitioners of the Tantra have understood this for aeons. Contrary to what many of us in western culture believe, eastern spirituality is not about denying or disdaining the body, its needs and its function. The body is not only acknowledged as the vehicle we use for mobility during our time on Earth, it is also actively used as part of the spiritual development process. The body is not denied or disdained, it is *disciplined*, which is something else altogether. In Eastern traditions discipline is not a harsh, punitive method of control, it is a loving practice built in to the daily routines of life, such as the practices of meditation and yoga.

By engaging our body in these regular disciplines from an early age it is educated not to run riot with cravings or to fall into sedentary habits. As a keen yogini, walker and swimmer myself I notice that my body craves some movement and exercise when I allow my mind to unbalance my life. The messages my body sends me get me out from behind my computer and back onto the beach, bringing everything back into harmony and balance. Magically, a gentle, regular physical exercise and meditation routine also brings the ubiquitous monkey mind into line. Is it healthy mind, healthy body or healthy body, healthy mind? I have found that it works both ways.

Those of you who have read and used my first book *You are Clairvoyant – Developing the Secret Skill We All Have* may remember the *Heart–Mind Balance* that enables you to bring harmony back to the dynamic between the way your heart would like to live your life and the way your head usually dominates it.

In this exercise – the 'Heart–Manifestation Balance' – you will discover how to bring balance back to what your heart needs and dreams of in your life and what you actually create in your physical reality. You will find that you can still keep a roof over your head and some money in the bank while bringing some of your dreams to fruition.

The 'Heart–Manifestation Balance' also gives you a little reality check around the difference between needs and wants. There is a massive difference between what we actually need in order to live safely, healthily and happily and what we want, or think we want. One of the clever tricks that we have played on ourselves in this consumer-based society has made millions of dollars for creators of products that would best be left on store shelves. We have come to almost totally believe that we 'need' things that we in fact only 'want'.

How many times have you or someone you know fallen prey to the belief that you 'need' a large car when a smaller vehicle would actually suffice, or a different outfit to wear every Saturday night, or that CD or DVD or computer game that you just 'had to have'? Then, to add insult to injury we go on to make ourselves unhappy when these false needs aren't fulfilled or work insane hours to pay for these unsatisfying wants. These are all symptoms of a mind out of control and out of balance with, or virtually disconnected from, the body it appears to conduct.

Earlier in this book we spoke about the power of the solar plexus chakra and its role in our intuitive guidance. Now we are going to harness its connection to our physical reality and our sense of identity in the world. The solar plexus chakra is the chakra of the 'I am' or the 'Self'. It is one step up from the navel chakra and its connection to family and tribe and two steps up from the base chakra and its connection to survival as a member of the entire human race. The solar plexus chakra is symbolic of your individual power and your connection to the physical and material world. When you link that energetically with the heart chakra and the creative energy of the navel chakra you can manifest beautiful things into your life.

The navel chakra, which is the third chakra involved in the 'Heart–Manifestation Balance' has a big role to play in your creativity, sexual energy, reproduction, the fluids of the body (except for blood which is governed by the base chakra) and your 'creative juices' as they are sometimes known. Working with the navel chakra makes this balancing process complete by helping you to manifest your heart's desires into physical reality *creatively*. Which in this context means, in your own, unique manner and with the steady guidance of your Intuitive Mind helping you all the way. Does that sound useful to you? Let's have a look at how it's done.

THE HEART – MANIFESTATION BALANCE

REQUIREMENTS: A place to sit or lie down comfortably. Peace and quiet.

OPTIONAL: Your journal and a pen. Gentle music, a candle, incense.
Anything you like to create a pleasant atmosphere.

TIME REQUIRED: 10 to 15 minutes

HOW OFTEN SHOULD I DO THIS? Regularly – once a week for example, is preferable to build up your 'creative manifestation muscle'.
Anytime you have a strong desire to manifest something beautiful into your life.

◆ **Your own Heart – Manifestation Balance:** this exercise can be done sitting up or lying down. Make sure you are comfortable, relaxed and attentive.

◆ Consider your intention to experience and enjoy a Heart–Manifestation Balance.

◆ Now focus on the following three chakras – the heart,

the solar plexus and the navel, and imagine a figure 8 connecting the three of them with the solar plexus chakra in the centre at the point where the figure 8 crosses over. Trace this figure 8 over your own body with your fingertips if you like to get a feel for where it sits, coming up from your navel chakra, crossing over at the solar plexus, looping up and around through the heart and then back down through the solar plexus again in the other direction, returning to the navel chakra and so on, in a continuous flow.

◆ Imagine that a stream or tube of constantly moving energy is flowing around this figure 8, pulsing up and down between the three chakras of its own accord. You may even feel the energy as it moves through you.

◆ Rest the palms of your hands on two of the three chakras. Whichever of them you feel drawn to is fine. Move one of your hands to the other chakra from time to time whenever you wish. Keep both of your palms on any two of the chakras for the duration of the balance.

Note: This is the energy pattern that you will be working with to create more balance and a stronger connection between your heart's desires and what you manifest into your physical reality. Just like blood is constantly circulating through your arteries and veins, you are now creating a pattern to allow energy to keep flowing through this circuit that connects these three chakras.

In most people the colour and quality of this energy is greyish, murky and sluggish the first time they use this technique. If you are always feeling rushed and stressed, the flow of energy may feel very fast and have a hectic kind of quality. The solar plexus chakra may feel anxious, tight or busy, while the navel chakra may feel heavy or blocked. The heart chakra can sometimes feel empty, emotional, frustrated or cramped and blocked. In some people it has a dreamy or airy quality – they may have lots of wistful ideas but find it difficult to make the real thing happen in their lives.

◆ Take a minute or two to notice what qualities you feel in your own chakras and how the energy is flowing around the figure 8. Don't try to analyse what you pick up, just focus on the process.

◆ Let your hands be the vehicles for a healing energy and Light that flows down to you from the Universe. Picture a beautiful, rich orange light flowing from your palms directly into the chakras you are touching.

◆ Send this energy and light into the chakras and feel it flow up and down through the entire figure 8, clearing away the dull colour and any blockages, and getting the energy moving more consistently or calming it down to a nice gentle flow. Stay with that for at least five minutes or until you feel that the energy is moving well and that the colour is lovely and bright.

Note: because of the constant challenges we face in bringing our heart's desires into reality we often put a great deal of strain on our solar plexus chakras. The sense of Self connected to this chakra is also concerned with how other people perceive us. When the creativity of the navel chakra meets the dreams and ideals of the heart chakra the solar plexus chakra will try to transform them into a practical pattern that best matches your image or ego-based version of yourself. Thus I often hear people saying things like: 'I would simply love to do such-and-such but I don't dare to'. In short, like the majority of people, they have learned how to conform in life, not how to follow their hearts.

For these reasons the solar plexus requires and receives a double dose of energy in this technique and is at the centre of this communication.

◆ Keep breathing deeply, moving your hands between your three chakras and visualising the orange energy and light flowing into them, and the figure 8, through your hands. If you sense that the bright healing colour is something other than orange that is absolutely fine, whatever colour comes to you is the colour to work with at this time and may vary from session to session.

◆ Imagine this beautiful energy flowing in to your three chakras. Feel your solar plexus becoming calm and balanced, your heart becoming clear and confident and the creativity from your navel chakra stirring and coming back to life. Stay with it until you feel you are glowing from within!

◆ When you are ready take your hands away and rest them by your sides, then picture yourself being surrounded by a beautiful cocoon of silver, gold or white light.

◆ If you wish you may make a few notes in your journal about what else you noticed during this exercise. Write down anything you feel you might like to refer back to in the future.

I normally feel great after giving myself a Heart – Manifestation Balance, so I hope you do too and you may be interested to know that just because you have ended the session it does not mean that the energy will disappear. The Heart – Manifestation Balance will keep on working for you for several hours, and if your Angels and Spirit Guides deem it necessary it may continue for several days. If you make the time to perform this simple technique regularly you will actually get to the point where you are simply topping yourself up. Regular practitioners of the Heart – Manifestation Balance will have a strong and beneficial connection between these chakras – a good working relationship so to speak. The connection can never be too good or work too well for you, so why not give yourself a balance once a week?

After a little practice you can do it in bed at night as you drift off to sleep, before you get up in the morning, on the bus or train or even in a meeting. Which brings me to another important point. It is lovely to use your hands as described above, but if you wish you can simply visualise the process in your mind. As long as your intention is to give yourself a 'Heart – Manifestation Balance' you can do so effectively without placing your hands on your chakras.

Perhaps when you first try this exercise you will be worried that you didn't sense much at all or that you were imagining things. Please be patient with yourself and stay with it. As with any other skill you have learned in the past, you had to practise a little before you felt really confident. If you get lovely sensations and visions of colours during your first session that's great, but if that doesn't happen immediately, all you need is a little more time. It is your intention that is most important. If you are clear on that and set out to give yourself a Heart – Manifestation Balance, then that is precisely what will happen and you will reap the rewards whether you can see or feel what is taking place or not.

TREATING SOMEONE ELSE

REQUIREMENTS: A place for your friend to sit or lie down comfortably.

OPTIONAL: Your journal, pen, gentle music, candle and incense.

TIME REQUIRED: 10 to 15 minutes

HOW OFTEN SHOULD I DO THIS? Once you have practised the Heart – Manifestation Balance on yourself a few times and have an understanding of how it works, it is quite a simple technique to perform on someone else.

- Take a minute to explain to your recipient what it is about or have them read this chapter.

- Focus on your intention, which in this case is to give someone you care about a Heart – Manifestation Balance.

- Let go of your own opinions about their emotional state or their problems; the more impartial you are the better. Giving someone a treatment like this is not about you trying to fix them or their life, it is about you helping them to have the clarity and strength to help themselves.

- Ask your friend to lie down and close their eyes. Make sure that you can sit or stand comfortably alongside them, then place your palms gently on any two of the three chakras involved in this technique – the heart, solar plexus and navel.

- Imagine the cleansing orange light flowing down from the cosmos, into your hands and into the person you are working on.

Note: You are being the channel or vehicle for the energy and light, there is nothing else that you have to do. As human beings our job is not to be the actual healer, but to strive to be the clearest possible conduit for the healing energies that the Universe naturally provides.

- Allow the healing energy to flow to you and through you, into their chakras. It is wonderful if you can feel the spin of their chakras on the palms of your hands, or sense flow of the energy around their 'figure 8', but if you can't then please don't worry. As long as your intention is clear then the Universe will take care of the rest.

- Move your hands between the three chakras as you feel guided to do so; feel free to tell the person that you are working on what is happening as you work, or wait until you have finished and then exchange feedback.

- Ten minutes will be enough unless you really feel it would be best to work a little longer. When you are ready to finish, imagine yourself wrapping them in a lovely soft cocoon of white, silver or gold energy and light. Let them know you are finishing in this way.

◆ Then take your hands away and picture yourself standing under a waterfall of silver light. This rinses away any energy that you may have absorbed from your friend while doing this hands-on treatment.

◆ Encourage them to lie or sit quietly for a minute or two before getting up and then ask for some feedback about their experience. It can be very exciting to hear about how soothing they found the heat from your hands or how they saw colours while you worked on them.

The suggested manner of working with the healing energy and light in this chapter is just one simple approach. If you have already learned how to channel Universal energy, either from my first book *You are Clairvoyant – Developing the Secret Skill We All Have* or through learning a modality such as Reiki, then you will know what to do, or can try the method described here. The important thing is that you are creating a clear and fresh communication and balance between these three vital chakras that will help you and the people you love manifest their heart's desires into reality.

When performing the 'Heart – Manifestation Balance' for yourself you should bear in mind that your heart usually knows what is best for you and to leave space in your thoughts for what it longs to manifest into your life. You may well wish to manifest a larger home, a new job or a relationship and there is no reason why you should not have any and all of those things if that is what you truly want.

Your heart, however, may lead you in directions that you had not dared to consciously consider or that your Monkey Mind might have quashed long ago. By all means focus on what it is that you believe you want while connecting these three chakras with each other in this manner, and aim high. Even your dreams may be small in scope compared to what the Universe can deliver, so it is a great idea to sometimes give yourself this balance with no particular want or need in mind, on an ongoing and regular basis. It will strengthen the influence that your heart's desires have on your life and help to create magic.

When you attend to your chakras in this way, with no agenda, you are making space for creations beyond your current scope to conceive. You are putting trust in the Universe and in your Higher Self. The natural intelligence that is inherent in you will then manifest of its own accord and from its vast level of awareness, rather than being focused on and possibly limited by the dreams that are bound by a focus on the material life.

DIANA'S EXPERIENCE

I have thoroughly enjoyed giving myself a regular Heart – Manifestation Balance and I believe it has helped me become much clearer about what I need in my personal life.

My mother had always brought me up to believe that I must marry a man who was 'successful in business' as she put it; and openly expressed disapproval of any man I dated who didn't wear a suit and tie to work. She wanted me to marry a doctor or a lawyer and had very traditional views about marriage. Goodness knows I went out of my way to please her, but my marriage was never really what I wanted, even though my ex-husband was a good man. We just weren't that compatible.

Divorced and in my 50, I knew that it was time for a change. I started using the Heart – Manifestation Balance regularly, with my focus on attracting a great relationship. The first change I noticed was the heaviness in my navel chakra area began to dissipate. I had felt blocked in that part of my body for as long as I could remember. Then I started exploring my interest in art and took up some classes where I met some artistic men who interested me, When a lady I met at a ceramics class invited me to an African dance and drumming workshop my first thought was about how foolish I might look, but I went along anyway and that is where I met my lovely man.

Naturally there are other things in life that I would like to manifest so I still use this exercise regularly to help them along and because I love the idea of my energy flowing smoothly and my chakras being healthy.

Diana N.
Auckland, New Zealand

CHAPTER EIGHTEEN

You Are Inspiring

Ordinary riches can be stolen, real riches cannot. In your soul are infinitely precious things that cannot be taken from you.

OSCAR WILDE
AUTHOR AND PLAYWRIGHT
1854–1900

You may not know it, but throughout your life you have already been an inspiration to many other people. Sometimes this will have been obvious to you. Maybe you organised a charity fundraising event or lost a large amount of weight and got your fitness back, and people told you that they felt inspired by your efforts. I am, however, willing to bet that you have been inspiring many people throughout your life in many ways without being aware of it – on a daily basis in fact.

Perhaps someone at work admires the way you handle a difficult colleague or that you have treasured photographs of your family and friends on your desk. Perhaps your neighbours love the way you keep your garden looking so lovely or always remember to drop a Christmas card into their letterbox. It might be your talent for whipping up a great meal at a moment's notice or how you always have time to pick up your friend's children from school when he is held up at work. Maybe you are a good joker or story teller or have travelled to many fascinating destinations.

As you go through life it is almost impossible to be aware of the impact you have on other people, or why they still remember you even after you haven't seen them for years. Like most people, you probably pay far too much attention to your perceived shortcomings or the things you haven't achieved yet. The fact is that we all have less than flattering qualities, but no matter who you are or what you do, you *are* an inspiring person.

I find people who do jobs like check out at the supermarket, driving public buses and working in hospitals and homes to be inspiring because they do work that I know I would not be able to do. I admire their daily strength, patience and courage.

I admire parents who talk to their children with respect and take the time to explain things to them, and parents who make sure that their children don't run riot in public places like restaurants. I am inspired by people who have overcome a poor education, early childhood trauma, or material disadvantage and have gone ahead and found things to be grateful for in life. I am uplifted by people who are flexible and find the opportunities in a new situation even when it wasn't exactly what they wanted. I am frequently touched by the generosity of my friends and always inspired by the courage, wisdom and determination of my clients and students.

One of the easiest ways you can inspire others is to simply share your life experiences with them. If you were to take our culture the way it is presented in the news media you could be forgiven for believing that complaining about absolutely everything has become a national pastime. How nice it is to hear a story from someone about something positive they do with their time, or the wonderful attitude that they have. In fact, a person who simply focuses on the positive and remains optimistic is very inspiring. Remember it is often the little things in life that inspire people and can go on to have a big impact.

You are an inspiring person in your own unique way and for that you deserve some positive feedback. Discovering how you inspire others will spur you on, especially during those times when you feel a little low. If you feel down you can turn your thoughts to the positive effect that you have on other people and remind yourself that you are appreciated and noticed. All you have to do now is ask them ...

YOU ARE INSPIRING

Requirements: Quality time to chat with your friends and family.

Optional: Your journal and a pen or a recording device. A nice café or a bottle of champagne to share.

Time required: This one is up to you!

How often should I do this? At least once and whenever you want to find out how you inspire the people in your life.

♦ **The Conversation** – Make a date to have a face to face conversation, or telephone conversation with three people you like, admire and trust. In person is fantastic if you can manage it, but if one of the people you wish to speak with lives far away the phone or video link via the internet is great.

♦ When making the date be sure to let each person know that you will be asking them about the times when you have inspired them in some way, giving them a day or two to think about it. Some people can come up with great answers when asked on the spot, but most people will remember more if they are given a little time beforehand.

- Then really listen to what they say and take their words to heart. Be aware of any tendency you may have to diminish or reject the positive feedback and compliments.

- Make a few notes in your journal about what they say, but don't let that activity distract you, *especially* if you are the type of person who feels awkward when receiving compliments. This is no time to bury your nose in your journal. If you are concerned that you will forget some of the nice things they'll say then take a recording device along instead. Yes, really! It's amazing what you can forget after only a few days.

- Make sure to let the others know they are being recorded and confirm that it is for your use only.

- Let the good feedback sink in, absorb and enjoy being honoured by people who like and care about you. Allow their words to inspire you and see yourself in an even better light.

- This may happen spontaneously anyway, but once they are finished showering you in good vibes maybe you can let your conversation partner know how they inspire you, or suggest that you make another date so that you can give him or her the same feel-good treatment.

- Have a laugh, shed some tears, enjoy this new level of communication and openness. Take some time to bask in the glow.

This is such a fun exercise and can be very revealing, even touching. It can take your friendships and relationships to a whole new level. We all love to know that we are noticed and appreciated, so isn't it time you had a wonderful treat like this? Many of my clients report that feeling unappreciated is one of the most hurtful things they deal with in life. It would be nice if we were all more forthcoming with compliments and thanks, but even when it comes your way do you really *hear* it? Like most people, you probably do hear the words in a physical sense, without allowing yourself to fully absorb them. This exercise is an opportunity to do just that.

Some of my students and clients have even brought their chosen three people together for one big conversation. This can work very well when they all know each other as they tend to egg each other on and it's a lot of fun. Most people prefer to do it one on one so that they can take it all in and focus on what that special person has to say. Whichever way you choose to proceed is fine as long as you do it and enjoy the warm words that you so obviously deserve. Go ahead, don't be shy or miss this opportunity out of some sense of false modesty. Tell your friends that you are reading this book and that the crazy author absolutely insists that you do this exercise, because I do!

Beverley's Experience

One of the most inspiring people in my world is someone I hardly know at all. He is an elderly gentleman (even older than me!) who walks with a very pronounced limp. I love going out for a walk most days and finally I could not keep my curiosity to myself. I said hello, commented on the beautiful sunny morning and we began to chat.

Turns out that about ten years ago, this man's wife died, he lost his job and then had a serious car accident, which was the cause of his limp all in the space of just twelve months. He told me how much it meant to him to stay fit, even though he would need his walking stick for the rest of his life; and how much he enjoyed meeting other people while out on his walks. He said life had been very good to him overall and that he wasn't going to sit at home feeling sorry for himself. I didn't realise it until he told me, but he said that he usually walks twice a day!

To me, this man is very inspiring. He had all the reasons in the world to feel bitter and let his health fade away, but there he was walking his little dog and chatting with anyone who had the time to stop, including me. I truly believe that all of us can inspire others in our own simple way and that it is important and uplifting to recognise your personal contribution.

Beverley J.
Hobart, Australia

CHAPTER NINETEEN

ARE ALL YOUR DUCKS FLYING IN THE SAME DIRECTION?

The road to success is always under construction.

ANONYMOUS

When I first heard the expression about having all your ducks flying in the same direction I laughed out loud. The image of a row of ducks flying along in a nice straight line – like those ceramic ducks people used to have on their walls – popped into my mind. It illustrated perfectly the meaning of harmony and unison. In years gone by it felt to me like my ducks were flying all over the place, which was symptomatic of the fact that I was not very clear on who I was or what I was doing with my life. In fact, some of my ducks were in direct contradiction to each other, flying in opposite directions.

Now I don't know about you, but living that way can be quite exhausting after a while. Having your ducks fly hither and thither can make it look like you are doing a lot, but generally your return on effort will be low. One of the ways the Universe confirms to me that I am staying on track is that people continually offer to help me and make my journey through life easier. When I moved house recently, for example, *six* friends willingly gave up a whole day to come and help. We were all done by lunchtime and spent the rest of the day enjoying ourselves. It all fell into place so beautifully and yet in the past, when my inner ducks had been squabbling, I often found it difficult to get help with anything.

The analogy created by our fine feathered friends is another way of asking if you are in harmony with yourself, your goals, who you say you are and who you would like to evolve into. This is a question worth asking yourself from time to time. The willingness to commit to your life and to exercise your power of choice are key factors in creating harmony in your life and those topics are covered in their own chapters. In this chapter we are going to take you through an exercise that will bring you into alignment on your spiritual and emotional levels.

People who meditate regularly often tell me that they have created a peaceful place in their mind, perhaps a relaxing scene like a beach or cosy room, and they take themselves there as soon as they realise that they are feeling stressed and need to calm down. They don't need to go off and sit cross-legged somewhere for half an hour, they just picture themselves sitting in their peaceful place and it takes them straight into that feeling. It can be the same with this exercise.

The inner vision and feeling of being totally aligned and in harmony with yourself is an awesome tool to use whenever you need to bring yourself back to *your* centre. It can help you avoid extremes of behaviours that may be debilitating or destructive.

Before undertaking the following exercise, please take a day or two to consider your current situation and how your key personality aspects are flying. In this way you can start to identify some aspects of your life which may be out of balance. Some key aspects might be your Relationship Aspect, your Career Aspect, your Parenting Aspect, your Creative or

Artistic Aspect, your Hobby Aspect, your Spiritual Aspect, your Health and Fitness Aspect, your Community Aware Aspect, your Social Aspect, your Financial Aspect and so on. As you can see all I am really doing is naming various areas of life that we tend to apportion out time and energy to.

An example of someone whose aspects are not harmoniously aligned may be a person who genuinely wants to stay in their committed relationship (Relationship Aspect) but who works extremely long hours, always takes on more work instead of letting others know they are too busy already, and then comes home too tired to spend meaningful time with their partner. That same person may also believe that they want to stay fit and healthy, but the Career Aspect may also be getting in the way of that. A person with well-aligned aspects can still work hard and do well in business, but they also take care to look after their health and put time with their partner firmly into their routine.

The focus of this exercise is to help you bring all your 'selves' into alignment with the goal of living an inspired and inspiring life. It's about creating inner harmony and balance rather than the inner conflict many people struggle with. By realigning yourself in this way you will be able to notice the aspects of your behaviour that are out of alignment with your overall direction in life and can help you to return more easily to that centre.

COMING BACK TO CENTRE

REQUIREMENTS: Your journal and a pen; then peace and quiet.

OPTIONAL: Gentle music, a candle, incense. Anything to help you create a relaxing atmosphere.

TIME REQUIRED: 10 to 15 minutes.

HOW OFTEN SHOULD I DO THIS? Whenever you need to bring yourself back to who you really are.

◆ After you have given yourself a couple of days and nights to sleep on it and mull it over, take your journal and write down the major aspects of you that operate in your life. Especially the ones that are being neglected at the moment, such as your Hobby Aspect. Perhaps you usually put work commitments before your personal life, so your Relationship or Intimacy Aspect may be way off in the background. Or in the case of a full time parent or carer it may be your Career Aspect that is being left out in the cold.

◆ Once you have completed your list leave that page open on the table or floor in front of you, just in case you need to sneak a peek at it during this process.

◆ Close your eyes and relax. Remind yourself of your intention to bring all these selves of yours into alignment so that you can live life from your core or centre.

◆ Now imagine all your different Aspects assembling around you. It could feel rather rowdy as they all jostle for space, or maybe they are quiet and orderly. However they behave is completely fine and is meant to be unique to you.

Note: please don't struggle with trying to 'see' them. If you are a naturally visual person and have a good imagination you might see your Aspects in your mind's eye or inner vision. There is your Career Aspect all dressed for work and there is your Hobby Aspect ready for a stint of gardening. It is lovely if you can get a sense of what your Aspects look like but this process will work just as well for you either way.

What is more likely is that you will feel the presence of your Aspects as you focus your attention on each one. Going through your list and closing your eyes to connect with each Aspect is another way. As long as your intention is to have them all gather together you will do fine.

So often a student will say to me, "Oh I couldn't see anything, I am not very visual" and yet when I ask them how their process went and what Aspects showed up they will frequently start describing the way they appeared. "My Hobby Aspect looked so happy; I had my big straw hat on and had a shovel in my hand." Suddenly realising what they have just said the student understands that they have been able to use their imagination as an illustrating device all along.

Seeing clairvoyantly is like seeing in your mind's eye, not like seeing a physical object in front of you. So just relax and work with your thoughts, feelings and images, however they come.

- When you feel that all of your Aspects are present, visualise yourself gently taking control of the situation. Ask them all to form one straight line in whatever order they choose. You are like the teacher at the front of school assembly or even the conductor of an orchestra.

- Notice if any of your Aspects barge towards the front, perhaps pushing others out of the way. Notice which Aspects face in a different direction or don't get into line at all. The act of lining up itself is not a disciplinary measure, it is simply a way for you to gauge which way all of your ducks are flying and whether or not your ducks are in unison.

- If you would like to, quickly jot down anything important you notice as you go.

- Allow your Aspects enough time to assemble themselves as well as they are willing and able to at this time. Don't try to analyse the whys and wherefores of their assembly, just take it all in for now.

- Once you feel that you have the gist of which Aspect is where please take a moment to write any important points or realisations in your journal. What have you realised about yourself during this experience?

◆ Finally, if you feel there is a particular Aspect that you would like to bring to the fore or if you would like to offer your group of Aspects some words of guidance or encouragement, please close your eyes again and do that.

◆ In your mind or speaking out loud, invite the important Aspect that is taking a back seat to come up to the front of the line. Or simply ask all your Aspects to work together more coherently and remind them that they are all on the same team. Focus on a sense of harmony and unity and picture your Aspects responding to this intention.

◆ Make any notes in your journal you feel are important and relevant and make a gentle commitment to yourself to notice and nurture any neglected Aspects a little more from now on.

I find this inner journey such a fascinating one and I enjoy using it whenever I feel the need to check in with myself. Life is a bit like sailing; you know where your journey began and where you would like to arrive but because the tides, winds and ocean are always in a state of flux you must always make time to consult your charts and reset your course. Real life ducks would have no qualms about doing that if a strong crosswind blew them off course. So why not give yourself the same leeway to adjust and bring yourself back on course whenever you wish.

The real benefits of this particular process emerge after you have done it, sometimes unfolding over weeks or months. Noticing how certain Aspects dominate while others hide their light, or how some of your Aspects actually want to go in a different direction, may cause you to make some adjustments to your daily life. Some relatively minor, some profound.

Rachel's Experience

I have always been very self-critical and have a fear of getting things wrong and being criticised by others. I have high standards and can be a bit too black and white about life. Doing this exercise helped me to see that I always expected myself to know where I was going and to charge ahead to that place without question. It took a lot of energy to drag myself back from that defeated place and it was often blown out of proportion. Close friends would tell me everything would work out fine or that I hadn't messed up to the extent I believed, but I just couldn't see it.

After doing the 'Coming Back to Centre' exercise a couple of times in the space of around a week I noticed my Rest and Relaxation Aspect and could feel how neglected and exhausted it was. I didn't see it really, although I had a flash of myself looking tired and grey; it was more of a feeling that this part of me and my life was barely hanging in there.

Once I had that experience I talked to my R&R self and my Intuitive Mind and came up with a few simple strategies. I now have a massage once a month, booked up to six months in advance. I also have a regular healing session with BelindaGrace, which helps me feel nurtured. When my girlfriends invite me away for the weekend I actually go and I check in regularly to make sure all my little ducks are happy.

It sounds so simple now that I have got the fuller picture, but I was working myself into the ground. My R&R Aspect loves being around people, relaxing, having fun and being pampered, but my Career Aspect was blocking it for fear it might take over. When I do this exercise it's as though all these aspects of myself realise that they are part of my team and that there is only one side they can be on. I love the feeling of balance it has brought me and the fact that I can allow myself to have a break in the knowledge that my play time helps me to be more effective in every area of my life.

RACHEL B.
CAIRNS, AUSTRALIA

CHAPTER TWENTY

THE POWER OF CHOICE

*When we acknowledge that all of life is sacred and that each act is an act of **choice**, then life is a sacred dance lived consciously each moment. When we live at this level, we participate in the creation of a better world.*

AUTHOR UNKNOWN

Earlier in this book I spoke of the concept of magic wands and the fact that they do exist. The Angels and Guides sometimes say that we are always running here and there looking for that special thing, that one thing that is going to help us solve all our problems. Usually we imagine that it needs to be something complex or impressive in order to be able to do the job, but it is actually right here with you all the time. The magic wand is choice, the power of which is always in your hands.

Choice is the magic wand that we have all been searching for; it is at the forefront of everything we experience in our lives. Right now you are choosing to discover new methods of connecting with your intuitive and clairvoyant guidance. You could choose to put this book down, never finish it and go watch a soap opera on television instead; but you have chosen to spend your time doing this and it will have a certain impact on your future. Every choice we make has an impact on what we perceive as our future. Again and again my Angels and Guides emphasise that there is no 'the future', meaning that there is no set script. What shows up in your future is a result of the probable realities you are creating through the choices you are making in this moment. It all comes back to the now.

A simple example might be when a client comes to me for a reading and asks if the building of their house will go well. The response they normally get will be along the lines of asking them what choices they have made so far.

Are they well organised, have they been realistic about the budget, do they understand enough about the process or do they need a project manager to supervise, what have they put in place that is going to affect the building of their home and what have they left to chance?

So you see, the Angels and Guides are very practical too, they won't just say: 'Oh yes, everything will be fine, sit back, put your feet up and don't worry.' They want you to understand that all the choices you make on a daily basis are the ingredients that come together as the smorgasbord of your life.

The most common reaction people have to the concept of choice as the magic wand is to point out all the things in their life they didn't choose. But even in those situations the power of choice is all important. We all inherit certain traits from our parents and ancestors, for instance, or you may be dealing with a difficult health situation or even life-threatening illness, or a situation or person that is 'not of your choosing'. In these cases it is the attitude you choose to have and how you choose to respond that makes all the difference. Inspiring people like Ian Gawler, who was given only a brief time to live by his doctors when diagnosed with cancer, chose to review his whole lifestyle and conquered his cancer through meditation and a wholistic approach to his health. Many years later he is vibrantly alive, leads the Gawler Foundation, runs cancer recovery programs, lectures all around the world and so much more. The way he chose to react to a situation that was not of his conscious choosing made all the difference to his life, literally.

Acknowledging that you always have a choice is the first step and becomes a very powerful tool in your quest to live an inspired and inspiring life. In the broader context the word choice will also mean 'attract' or 'manifest'. If you are regularly attracting or manifesting situations, experiences and people that you believe are not of your choosing it's just the Universe's way of letting you know that you are out of harmony with yourself. Nothing in life is accidental, so if the same old stuff keeps recycling in your life you may need to investigate your past lives, have a chakra balance, take up some regular exercise, get some professional counselling and do whatever it is you need to do to let go of those particular patterns.

Accepting that you have the power of choice requires a level of spiritual and emotional maturity. To choose to use that magic wand directly implies that you are willing to take responsibility for your choices and what they create. This kind of power comes with responsibility of a positive nature, as all true wizards know. It's a matter of no blame and lots of gain because – you know what? If you aren't thrilled with what one choice creates in any given moment, you have the opportunity to choose again. Remind yourself of what my Angels and Guides always say: there is no such thing as a mistake, only experience and experiment. Seeing your life like that is a choice as well.

The time has come to use your magic wand consciously so that you can live your inspired and inspiring life. It is the fastest way out of debilitating behavioural patterns such as being a rescuer, pleaser, hero or victim, and don't we all know what it feels like to be any or all of those sometimes! Just like my client Jessica who realised that the power of choice is always in her hands. She was continually getting involved in destructive relationships, choosing to hold her tongue rather than speak up for herself, pretending that her feelings and needs didn't really matter and that she would get what she wanted next time. Now she acknowledges that everything is a choice – whether to say yes or no, whether to agree or disagree, whether to speak up in the moment or remain silent, whether to go along with what others expect or do what she feels is best for her. Jessica now knows that while some of these events may seem minor at the time, each one is a powerful turning point. She has chosen to become increasingly aware of these moments and is learning how to utilise them to create the kind of life she can be proud of.

One of the most important things you can do while you are re-learning your choice skills is to slow down. As you go through your day, take time to notice all the choices you are making. Slow down and, rather than just reacting or responding in your usual way, give yourself permission to think things over, sleep on it and say to people, 'I need some time to consider that, to get in touch with my feelings about it. I will get back to you tomorrow or when I am ready.'

There is something I got into the habit of doing many years ago that you might find useful. At the end of the day, even as you are lying in bed before you go to sleep, reflect on the events of your day and notice when your choices were in line with your goals and who you really are and when they weren't. This simple process of daily reflection can bring about some interesting ah-ha moments. The more aware you become of how you tend to make choices, the times you feel under pressure and the times you choose well, the more likely you are to make increasingly constructive choices in the future. In every choice, no matter how large or small, you have the opportunity to steer yourself further along your highest and most harmonious path. The following exercise will help you to connect to your intuitive guidance and what feels best for you.

CHOOSING YOUR HIGHEST PATH

REQUIREMENTS: A quiet place where you can sit comfortably.

OPTIONAL: Your journal and a pen. A candle, incense, gentle music.
Anything you like to create a pleasant mood.

TIME REQUIRED: 10 to 15 minutes.

HOW OFTEN SHOULD I DO THIS? Any time you would like to make an intuitive choice.

◆ Sitting comfortably, close your eyes and take a few minutes to contemplate the situation before you. Consider all the options that you believe are realistic and you would be willing to follow through. If writing things down is helpful to you then use your journal to make a succinct list of your options.

Note: this technique is useful at any time in your life. Initially I would encourage you to use it for what you regard as smaller choices, such as which restaurant to go to on the weekend or whether or not to accept an invitation of some kind. Use it any time you feel some sort of hesitation or confusion, and especially if your Money Mind is going back and forth like a ping-pong match trying to figure out the pros and cons. Once you have a little experience then you can start using it to help you make more momentous choices such as whether or not to leave your job or get married, for example. It's your life, so you can leap straight in with the big questions if you like, but that is what my team recommends!

- Allow the various options to clarify themselves so that the clutter of what other people might think and all the 'what-ifs' can fall away.

- Now picture yourself standing on a pathway or roadway in a beautiful, peaceful setting – out in the countryside, surrounded by green fields and rolling hills perhaps. The road of your life so far stretches out behind you and the options related to the choice you are contemplating now fan out before you as forks or branches in that road.

- Mentally label all of the branches so that each one represents one of your options.

Note: you will find that some situations offer quite a few possible choices while in other situations you may feel it's either-or; in which case there would be a branch going off to the left and another off to the right. In the case of multiple options you will see or sense that number of branches in the road. If there are more than six options or branches you may need to go back and look at the situation again in order to break it down into simpler elements. For example people often try to bundle a number of decisions into one big decision, such as "My partner has just proposed to me. Should I say yes, should I move in with him now or wait till we get married, should we get married here or in my hometown … ???" You can see how that would be too much to tackle in one go, yet it is amazing how often we put pressure on ourselves to sort everything out in one swoop. Make sure you are focusing on one choice at a time and the whole process will be much more effective.

- Now ask your Intuitive Mind to highlight the best option for you. Take your awareness or attention to your heart chakra and tune in to your feelings rather than becoming distracted by your thoughts.

- Be patient. Sit, breathe, relax and keep gently asking your Intuitive Mind to clearly point out your highest choice.

Note: the way in which your highest choice will be highlighted for you will be unique to you and may vary from one process to the next. Some people feel a sensation like a physical pull in the direction that is best for them. Those who are more visual report seeing the preferred path light up as though some clouds have parted and the sun is shining down on that particular branch alone. Sometimes my Intuitive Mind will give me the answer verbally, like a clear thought popping into my mind and I will hear the words such as 'go now' or 'wait'. When the answer comes it is also likely that you will feel it in your body as a sense of knowing or calm. As with all things, practice makes perfect, so be patient with yourself as you learn how to communicate with your intuitive guidance once more.

- Once the preferred choice has been indicated to you take a few more moments to notice how you feel about that option. Don't start to analyse it, just notice your feeling response.

◆ Thank your Intuitive Mind for its guidance and open your eyes.

◆ Write the choice shown to you in your journal if you wish.

Now you have your answer the only choice you have to make is whether or not you are going to follow that guidance. This is possibly the greatest challenge that we all face when working with our own intuitive and clairvoyant awareness. If you allow your Monkey Mind to step in and start telling you all the reasons you should not proceed, then you may not go ahead with that option. It's your choice. No one else can stand in your shoes and following the path of the heart does take courage sometimes. Be patient with yourself and remember if you choose to let rationale and logic win out this time that's not necessarily a bad thing, as long as you take the time later to reflect on the results your choices created. Slowly and surely you will learn to trust your intuitive guidance and act on it more. The pace at which you do this must be your own and, as you know, you will always get a chance to choose again next time.

LESLEY'S EXPERIENCE

Maybe it's because I'm a Libran that I found it so difficult to make decisions, even seemingly trivial ones. I started using this technique a few months ago, and to be honest I didn't expect any earth shattering results. At first I did look at the simpler questions in my life so that I could get a feel for how my Intuitive Mind might show me the way. Sometimes it was frustrating and I wasn't sure if I had been given an answer or not. When that happened it was usually because I was already attached to wanting a particular answer and wasn't really open to what my inner wisdom wanted to show me.

I continued to practise though because my life-long problem with indecisiveness was driving me around the bend. After a bit of experimentation and including the use of my journal, I found this process started to work well. Practising and being patient with myself was definitely worth it because the old anxiety is gone; my job, as I now see it, is to hand the task of choosing over to my Intuitive Mind and then to follow that guidance to the best of my ability. This process has taken so much of the stress of choosing and change out of my life and helped me to develop my confidence.

LESLEY G.
SYDNEY, AUSTRALIA

CHAPTER TWENTY-ONE

THE JOY OF MAKING IT HAPPEN

The moment one definitely commits oneself then providence moves too. All sorts of things occur to help one that would never have otherwise occurred. Unforeseen incidents, meetings and material assistance which no one could have dreamed of now come your way.

MEISTER ECKHART
GERMAN PHILOSOPHER, SAGE AND MYSTIC
1260–1328

My Angels and Spirit Guides always say that there is no such thing as a mistake, only experience and experiment. Living an inspired and inspiring life has a lot to do with being willing to take that first step without being sure of where your journey will lead. If you wait for a guarantee that you will receive the outcome you want you may never get started. More often than we care to admit we actually have little idea and hardly any control over long term outcomes. The key to overcoming the anxieties this fact can arouse is to actually take those first small steps. In fact, starting something new is always beneficial in terms of learning and personal growth and there is always an excellent chance that everything will work out well.

One of my favourite movies is 'Miss Potter' about the wonderful author and artist Beatrix Potter. At the beginning of the movie she says that starting to write a new book is like embarking on an amazing new adventure, because she never knows where it is going to take her. The publication of her work led to some incredible experiences in her life. Some of them were along the lines of what an author might expect when her work becomes published and popular. Other experiences that came her way changed her life and view of it for ever, but if she had tried to anticipate or plan those things … well, that's the whole point, she could not have anticipated or planned them.

Anyone who knows me can easily understand why Beatrix Potter is so inspiring to me, she has so many characteristics I admire and her life was an amazing journey. I remember my own journey to finally getting published and how an unplannable sequence of events led me there. Years ago I wrote and published a book myself and through various channels I sold a few hundred copies. When I look back on it now, though, I can see that it was my commitment to writing and financing the publication of my own work that opened doors for me a few years later and led to me being asked to present a workshop at a wonderful bookstore here in Sydney. The workshop was a sell out; literally standing room only and all my remaining stock was sold. As I relaxed and chatted with the staff afterwards I mentioned that I had no more copies of my book left and would have to consider my next move. One of them asked me if I was looking for a publisher and the rest is history. I am very happy with the way things have worked out.

Being happy in life and creating things to feel inspired about is all about giving it a go. If I had talked myself out of all the effort and expense of writing and self-publishing my first book who knows where I would be now? The Universe has this uncanny way of designing things on your behalf when you are really committed to something, even and especially when you aren't exactly sure how you are going to achieve your original goals. I think it is so important to remember that so much more is possible than what our conscious minds can imagine.

Ultimately, it is vital to take the plunge in life. No amount of study, discussion or theorising can replace actual experience because it is out there, on the playing field, that you learn the most about yourself. Truly committing yourself to an activity, a goal or a way of life is an awesome way to inspire yourself and will play a big part in helping you to discover the things that bring a sense of meaning and purpose to you personally. I believe it was the American author Henry David Thoreau who said, 'Most men live lives of quiet desperation and go to their graves with a song still in them.' This statement might seem a little grim, but even so he does make us think about the consequences of allowing our hopes, dreams and aspirations to wither on the vine. Maybe it's time for you to look at where you might have let security become dull predictability and start to fill your life with exciting possibilities instead.

From what I have observed and been told by hundreds of people over the last few years, fear of failing seems to be the biggest obstacle. We absolutely need to redefine the meaning of failure. It's all about how you choose to see things. If you were an athlete who made it to the Olympic Games you could view yourself as a winner even if you came last in your event. You did something extraordinary with your life; you followed a dream and allowed yourself to excel at your own special talent. You had an amazing experience. Maybe you didn't go home with a medal, but hey, how many people do you know who have competed in the Olympics? Amazing as it may seem to us mere mortals, who may have trouble running around the block, some athletes have fallen into states of depression and self neglect after they 'failed' to win gold. They created and believed an idea that dictated a gold medal to be the only indication of success. As we can see, putting such narrow limits on the meaning of success can be detrimental indeed.

Perhaps you and I aren't going to be featured in the next Olympic squad, but so what? Success, fulfilment and the experiences of inspiration and satisfaction are available to everyone, everywhere, at all times. Finding meaning and purpose in life and living in an inspired way sometimes involves taking a chance on yourself. It's about having an attitude that is flexible and open to what shows up in response to your effort, rather than becoming downcast when things don't turn out exactly as you wish straight away. There are no guarantees in life, but there are many opportunities.

Committing yourself to something and seeing it through will always bring satisfaction, growth and an improved sense of self. Sometimes this will involve risking your time, money, pride, favourite ideas, feelings and even your self image; but no one is suggesting you take big risks or go from one extreme to the other. Planning, research and tuning in to your personal sense of what feels right are still important. One step at a time is a much better approach, and a healthy antidote to inertia. The challenging thing about life is that no one else can do it for you, but that becomes its own reward when you do finally get on your way. Just like the lion and the tin man in the *Wizard of Oz*, you *will* find that you have more courage and more ability than you ever dared believe possible.

Another fantastic approach to living an inspiring life full of discovery and adventure, which must be mentioned here, is the ability to laugh at yourself and at life. I often see people getting tense and upset about relatively minor things or something that has gone beyond their control. That kind of stress over every twist and turn in life is not worth all the energy and time you give it. Make a point of catching yourself out when you are becoming too serious or intense about something. Smile, take a deep breath and ask yourself if you could just back off or let go a little. Living in a rushed and fractious manner can often be more of a habit than a true reflection of your reality, and the fact is that you will handle your challenges more easily if you can lighten up and remind yourself that it's probably not a matter of life and death.

There is no evidence anywhere to suggest that life was ever meant to be serious. Certainly there are many things in life that are profound, touching, moving and, yes, sometimes even painful. I wouldn't encourage you to suppress the urge to cry, scream or curse if that is what you need to do to express your true feelings, but the pendulum should always swing back to the healthy centre, of which humour is the heart. No matter what it is that ails us, it will pass, and all the more quickly with laughter, which truly is our best medicine.

In my line of work I am constantly speaking with people who are experiencing major traumas and setbacks. Not a week goes by without a conversation about a divorce, a suicide or suicide attempt, severe depression, bankruptcy or other forms of financial difficulty, the death of a loved one, retrenchment and redundancy, infidelity, abandonment, mental health issues, drug and alcohol addiction, sexual abuse or illness and injury. The people who I notice recover most quickly from these very difficult situations are the ones who are committed to something. It could be that they want to get their health back so they can see their children and grandchildren grow up; or that they are determined to pay back their creditors after their business collapsed and re-establish a good name for themselves.

Whatever it is that you make a commitment to will spur you on and remaining cheerful through the minor challenges that come up on a daily basis will arm you with a spiritual toughness and resilience that is invaluable. You can always find something to laugh about, whether it's a memory of a funny incident, a great comedy that you saw at the cinema or the thought of someone who always makes you smile. Natural beauty and the antics of my cat Molly make me smile too, so usually all I need to do is have a Molly Moment or look out the window. Make sure you have at least a small collection of laughter-inducing or feel-good movies at home, some comic CDs in the car or a radio station that keeps things upbeat. Gravitate towards the quirky and the humorous rather than the negative and critical.

Gossip magazines and other forms of negative media should be kept to a minimum or avoided completely. They are shiny and colourful, so are therefore alluring, but so often they focus on the nasty and sordid aspects of life or just whip up a story if one doesn't really exist. The momentary buzz you may get from looking at those pictures of 'the beautiful people' is like a drug and you have to come down from it some time. The most common effect is you wind up seeing yourself as not good enough or your life dull and boring by comparison. Don't allow shallow gossip and artificially enhanced photos of people you don't even know to bring you down! The same goes for all those horrible crime shows that are so frighteningly popular these days. I find the trailers for these shows terrifying enough, never mind watching the whole program. All the characters in these shows are so self important, significant and serious. It's as though the fate of the world rests on their shoulders and as you watch these shows your stress levels go up. Flick over to a comedy or a nature documentary for a change, or put on one of your happy movies instead.

Gratitude for all that you have is the close companion of joy. When you think about the good things and the blessings in your life you are bound to smile, and when you recommit to your life and your dreams every day you will always have something to feel positive about.

HUMOUR AND COMMITMENT AND MAKING IT HAPPEN

REQUIREMENTS: Your journal and a pen, your sense of humour and some courage muscles.

OPTIONAL: Gentle music, a candle, incense. Anything that helps to create a pleasant mood.

TIME REQUIRED: 10 to 15 minutes for the journal section of the exercise.

HOW OFTEN SHOULD I DO THIS? Do the journal exercise at least once, and then whenever you feel like you may be drifting off your path. The remainder is something you can use for the rest of your life.

◆ **Part One: A lighter perspective** – With your journal to hand, sit and look back on your life. Recall some of the occasions during which your sense of humour and ability to see the lighter side helped you to deal with that experience. Write them down in as much detail as you wish.

◆ Next, consider some of the times in your life when you felt very stressed, upset, angry or hurt about something only to find out that things were much better than you originally thought. Take a moment to remember how the situation worked out so much more easily than you had expected and why you could smile or laugh about it later.

- Notice how much easier that experience would have been if you had remained lighter and calmer. Would you have had to go through all that stress, fall out with and then have to apologise to those people or whatever the case was? How could a sense of humour and a more trusting perspective have helped you back then? Write down your thoughts in your journal.

- **Part Two: Acknowledge the positive** – Look back on your life and note down at least one time when you really committed to something and you got a great result. Write down your memories of that experience and your feelings. Then, write down at least three things that you have always wanted to commit to doing but are still putting off due to fear of failure, rejection or looking foolish.

- Choose one, and then let at least one good friend know that you are going to commit to this new experience and ask them to support you. Do any necessary research and make whatever plans you feel are reasonable, then approach it with a sense of fun and adventure.

- **Part Three: Find your joy** – Laughter, humour and happiness are good for you, being around people who are not just talkers but doers is inspiring – seek them out!

◆ Find something to smile and laugh about every day.

Denice's Experience

I have always loved nice fabrics and was in seventh heaven when my first sewing machine was given to me on my seventh Birthday! From there my passion grew and I have been a member of a quilters group for as long as I can remember.

Some years ago we decided to make quilts for various charities in the Melbourne area. We love making them and thoroughly enjoy the socialising that naturally occurs when we all get together. Out of our initial idea we developed some themes for our charity quilts. The first is 'Quilts of Love' which are tiny quilts donated to the Royal Women's Hospital for mothers and their premature babies. Sadly, many of these babies don't survive long, so the quilt is something special for the parents to remember their special little angel by.

The second idea is 'Quilts for Cancer', which go to the local cancer hospice to brighten up the often dull and sterile décor and give those who are ill something to snuggle up in. 'Quilts for Kids' is the other theme and these quilts go to the local Community Policing squad and are given to children and teenagers who have been taken from violent and abusive homes. The idea is to give comfort to a young person in distress.

All the quilters donate their time, expertise and materials. Most of them are on pensions or only working part time, but this has never stopped them giving. I applied for a grant from the bank I work for and they gave us $2000 towards materials, which was a great help.

Now a friend and I are setting up a business designing beautiful fabrics especially made for quilting. We are drawing the designs ourselves and are going to have them printed professionally and sell them to quilters all around the world.

So you can see that it's not just the quilting itself that I find inspiring, it's the people I meet and mix with and the things that we manage to accomplish. I think it's possible to turn just about any hobby or interest into something beneficial. We have our own community and then we reach out and connect with the wider community in various ways. It's fun and very rewarding

DENICE S.
MELBOURNE, AUSTRALIA.

CHAPTER TWENTY-TWO

YOUR HEALTH IS
YOUR WEALTH

Health is a state of complete harmony of the body, mind and spirit. When one is free from physical disabilities and mental distractions, the gates of the soul open.

B.K.S. IYENGAR
BORN 1918
FOUNDER OF IYENGAR YOGA AND
AUTHOR OF NUMEROUS BOOKS ON YOGA,
SPIRITUALITY AND HEALTH

A reasonable level of health and fitness is the greatest asset you can have, but if a genie popped out of a bottle in front of you right now and offered you three wishes would it occur to you to put life-long health and fitness on your list? Unfortunately it is all too easy to take your health for granted, until it's compromised. In some ways this is actually quite natural as we are not meant to be aware of our organs, joints and so on, as we go about our daily business. A healthy body handles life effortlessly; it is only when there is pain or a problem that we suddenly notice the affected area. What usually happens, however, is that most of our loss of fitness and mobility comes on gradually, so we tend to ignore it, telling ourselves, 'I will definitely go to the gym/start that new diet/book into a yoga course soon.'

There are literally millions of methods you could use or experts you can refer to for advice on diet and exercise, so you don't need me to attempt to write another health and fitness regimen here. My only advice is to keep things simple and aim for balance in all things in your life. Deep down we all know what foods are good for us and what should be taken in moderation: anything else is just pretending.

A healthy body and a reasonable level of fitness may not be the ultimate cause of happiness in and of itself, but it will absolutely enhance your enjoyment of *every* area of your life. Without exception you will enjoy how much easier it is to do what you need to do when you are well; and all the things you *want* to do are brought within closer range. How can you walk the Grand Canyon, teach your kids to play football or make your garden look gorgeous when you are puffing, aching and struggling from the effort? You want to see those parts of the world you haven't been to yet, inspire your children and grandchildren to get outdoors and have fun and keep up hobbies that give your life meaning and purpose into a ripe old age.

Fit and healthy people are inspiring purely because they have more energy and enthusiasm and because, as Adrian O. said, your body is your spiritual processing plant. A healthy person actually has a higher vibration! Looking after your body and overall health is just as much a part of your spiritual development as meditating, reading books on the subject or having a session with your healer. In the West we have developed an attitude whereby we wait until there is something wrong before turning to our 'health' system to help us fix it. This is not a health system at all, but rather a system of fighting fires instead of taking easy and sensible steps to prevent them.

Nothing is more inspiring than having your optimum level of fitness, health and strength. Getting back to my commitment to my own health is one of the best things I have ever done and I don't need a doctor to tell me it has added years to my life. Being in good health opens the doors to fully experiencing a great life. Most people would ask the genie in the bottle for a large sum of money, a new home or a new car; perhaps even a soulmate. All excellent requests, of course, but as a healthy person you would have so much more fun and involvement when spending all that extra cash, decorating your new home, zooming around in your new car and making love to your sexy new soulmate. Good health makes everything in life better.

Before we move on to the magical little exercise my Angels and Guides taught me to use for good health and energy, I would like to encourage you to exercise – literally! Just thirty minutes at least four days a week is a small investment when you consider the fabulous returns. Walking, swimming, yoga, pilates, gardening, cycling, dancing, working in your local co-op store, walking dogs at an animal welfare centre or sweeping out animal shelters are all ways to make exercise interesting and fun. Make your form of exercise as sociable and rewarding as any wonderful idea your imagination can cook up. Enjoy your regular exercise not only as a way to keep fit but as something that will bring many more rewards into your life.

The following exercise is known as a Rejuvenation Treatment and is a simple process taught to me by my 'team' a few years ago. Since then it has become a favourite with me, my students and clients alike. I often use it when I feel tired and need to refresh myself; the Rejuvenation Treatment has helped me to accomplish whatever I needed to do on numerous occasions.

I love working with the bubbly golden energy and Light; it reminds me of champagne because it is that delicate golden colour and is literally bubbly and tingly.

It is a great treatment to use in stress situations also, such as when you are studying for exams and is great for tired eyes after staring at a computer screen for hours. The bubbly golden Light will also lift your mood, so if you have a tendency towards melancholy, feel a bit low or have a habit of looking on the pessimistic side of life, then the Rejuvenation Treatment will provide an excellent pep-up. It is cleansing and revitalising on all levels – mental, emotional, physical and spiritual – so treat yourself to a little cosmic champagne any time you like.

A REJUVENATION TREATMENT

REQUIREMENTS: A place to sit comfortably.

OPTIONAL: Gentle music, a candle, incense.

Anything that helps you create a pleasant atmosphere.

TIME REQUIRED: 5 to 10 minutes.

HOW OFTEN SHOULD I DO THIS? Daily if you wish as a regular treatment to boost energy and treat ailments, or whenever you feel you need it.

- Sit comfortably with the soles of your feet flat on the floor, your hands resting in your lap or by your side. Breathe deeply and consider your intention to give yourself a lovely Rejuvenation Treatment.

- Take a moment to imagine the centre of the Universe or Cosmos, whatever that may look like to you. See the planets and swirling galaxies fading away into the infinite distance.

- Visualise a stream of this bubbly, pale gold energy and Light flowing down from the centre of the Universe and coming gently down towards you and onto the top of your head. Imagine this Light flowing into your whole body through your crown chakra and over the surface of your body as well.

- Picture it bubbling and gurgling through every part of you, in between every cell and fibre of your physical form. If you have a headache or tired eyes then you can intend more of the golden light to go to those areas to clear away the fatigue and stress. Ask the Light to go to the areas of your body and energy field (aura) that need it most.

Note: the Rejuvenation Treatment is like a refreshing cleanse. If you are ill or have ongoing ailments such as joint pain you can use the Rejuvenation Treatment to gently flush those areas out. It is not a torrent, just a gentle, steady and refreshing flow. Let your imagination guide you through the process. It is also quite common to feel certain sensations while the golden bubbles are flowing through and over you. Some people will experience tingling sensations; others may feel cooler or warmer. There are no sensations that are better or more important than others, each person is different, just notice what happens for you without fixating on or analysing it. Most sensations only last a short while as the bubbly, golden Light soon rinses any toxins or blockages away.

- Continue to breathe in a deep and relaxed manner, keep your mind gently focused on the Light as it makes its way from the Cosmos to and then through and around you. Ask that it wash away any negative or superfluous worries or thoughts that may be weighing you down and then let it flow out through and over your legs and feet into the floor.

◆ Imagine our beautiful Mother Earth absorbing it all and drawing it all away. Feel the golden Light with its refreshing bubbles soaking into the earth beneath you. Stay with the process until you feel the last of the Light drain away and when you are ready, open your eyes.

◆ If you wish, you may also like to surround yourself in a cocoon of white energy and Light, or any other colour of your choice. Once your Rejuvenation Treatment is over you will feel refreshed and ready to get on with or continue your day.

As you can see, the Rejuvenation Treatment is quick and easy. Once you have tried it a couple of times you should have no problem calling on it whenever you need a lift.

Obviously it is a great treatment first thing in the morning or during a long day at work, university or school. Use it before an outing at night to help you stay alert or when you stop for a break during a long drive. The Rejuvenation treatment is not a substitute for appropriate health and sleep practices, but it will refresh and cleanse, and is far healthier and cheaper than too much coffee or expensive de-tox formulas. It's up to you to discover whether or not you can use this treatment before going to bed. Some people find that it does help them to have more restful sleep, while other people have reported that the Rejuvenation Treatment causes them to feel bright and awake and is therefore not conducive to sleep. It is important to remember that while the benefits of this treatment can be wide ranging, it is not a panacea for all ills. Use it as often as you like to help you with your busy lifestyle and support the other healthy practices you are committed to following.

Marjorie's experience

After my hip operation I thought my mobility would never be as good again. I think I talked myself into that idea too. Through BelindaGrace my Angels and Spirit Guides urged me to begin a gentle exercise routine and to build myself back up from there. I was not enthusiastic at first, I will admit, but I did it anyway because I didn't like to think about where my health was heading.

I gave myself a Rejuvenation Treatment three or four times a week and always enjoyed the experience of that bubbling, golden Light.

Now I look back on myself from that time and it's like seeing another person. I was rapidly becoming an old lady and depended on a walking stick. The walking stick is gathering dust now and I am thrilled. I use an exercise bike at home most days, love to go for a walk and can even manage the steep stairs down to the beach from my daughter's place as I love to have a swim whenever I visit her. I have my life back and am enjoying myself more than I ever thought possible at 73 years of age.

Marjorie H.
Outback New South Wales
Australia

CHAPTER TWENTY-THREE

LIVING AN INSPIRED AND INSPIRING LIFE

Try not to become a person of success, rather become a person of value.

ALBERT EINSTEIN
THEORETICAL PHYSICIST
1879-1955

It is my belief that the human race and the long journey we have all been on is now at the turning of the tide. All our problems aren't going to disintegrate over night, but I do feel that many of us are ready to do what we need to do in order to live from a place of love and openness instead of that closed place of fear. As an individual you are capable of great things and when you join with your friends, family and colleagues, the greatness of your ability grows exponentially.

The age that we are now moving into is one that we are all creating. There is no force in the heavens pulling all the strings. We are one with that unnameable, indescribable force because it is within us as well as around us at all times. This will be the era of leading by example rather than waiting for someone 'in power' to make it happen on our behalf, therefore it is also the era of inspired living on a personal and communal level.

All around you people will begin to overcome the great obstacles that have held them back for years, or even lifetimes. When you feel up to the task you may wish to extend a helping hand in order to assist them with their progress, knowing as you do how it feels to be in that place. At other times it will be you or I reaching out for some support, some helpful advice based on experience and a willingness to listen without being judged. We can all leap-frog each other on the way to enlightenment and enlightened living; making bridges and stepping stones of our own experience and learning to share with each other. We may have lost the know-how it takes to live in small tribes but we can still benefit from one aspect of tribal culture at least – everybody making a contribution to society, no matter how old or young, how frail or strong, no matter what gender. We all have a part to play and nobody gets left behind.

The way we educate ourselves and especially our children needs to evolve dramatically. Not a moment too soon will we start to teach them to be proud of their uniqueness and individuality. Let us create a world in which letters after our names and dollars in our bank accounts are not the main measure of our success. Living an inspired and inspiring life, living a life filled with meaning and purpose is about being a person of value, with values to live by and the willingness to value ourselves and others. Your journey is unique. There has never been anyone exactly like you in the entire history of the human race and there never will be again. Think about that for a moment and then dare to be the individual you already are. Measure your successes in life by the number of times you were willing to try something new, to ask a question and to step outside your comfort zone just a little.

Instead of waiting for the world to come to your doorstep with the whole package neatly wrapped up and tied with a bow, with directions clearly detailed on a map, why don't you go out there and explore? Be curious about what life may have to offer, because imagining that you already know what is going to happen, that you know what is out there or that you have seen it all just isn't so. A blasé or cynical attitude is like death to the mind and the soul, and if you are afflicted by those attitudes seek help until you can let go of those ways of seeing the world. Getting inspired about life is about looking at your world with new eyes every day.

Remember to be gentle with yourself and the world. We all make mistakes and we are all doing the best we can with the level of consciousness we have. The minute one person raises their level of consciousness and awareness is the minute in which the bar is raised for all of us. When you do your share the Light from your little candle shines out to help illuminate all of the world, and it's all of our candles combined that will make the difference. Do whatever it is you need to do in order to forgive yourself and others for any wounds you have suffered in the past and stop trying to live in the future, because nothing impedes growth of consciousness and your connection with your Intuitive Mind more than not living in the present.

Commit to being responsible for creating your own future through what you are thinking, saying, choosing and doing in this moment, and recognise that those things are the building blocks of all the probable realities you are setting up as your possible futures. Stop telling yourself that if only you had had such-and-such in the past you would be a better person today; or that today is no good but that hopefully things might be better tomorrow. Grab life by the throat instead and make it so. Seek out mentors, counsellors, teachers, peers and friends who can help you to realise your full potential. Openly acknowledge and appreciate all that is good about your life and bless them; because each time you do you send an energy out into the Universe that brings more of the same back to you.

Learn to keep your own life, needs, concerns and wants in perspective. There is no reason why you shouldn't have all the delights that this world has to offer, yet paradoxically, you will enjoy them more when you don't *have to have them*. Remind yourself that if some people don't seem very interested in you or don't want to do things your way it's not the end of the world. Try standing in their shoes for a while or just put your head down and get on with the business of your own evolution. Sometimes it's just not about you, and you need to gather your spiritual resilience around you and get on with your life.

Treat this book as a workbook. Use it, re-use it and scribble all over it if you need to. Many people come to me after reading my first book and say, 'I read your book in a couple of days, I really enjoyed it.' My first response is to thank them and my second is usually something like: 'It is a very simple book certainly and easy to read, it is the kind of book you *can* read in two days and yet work with for a lifetime.' Believe me, you can never become too attuned to your own higher wisdom; and after twelve years of working as a Clairvoyant Healer I have been shown many times that just when I thought it couldn't get any more amazing and the guidance could not be any more sublime, they take me to the next level and it is.

Living an inspired and inspiring life is actually quite simple once you allow it to begin. The most difficult part is getting all the clutter out of the way first so your can see your path more clearly. Let this book be one of the tools you use to help you put your feet on your pathway again. Read the whole book in two days if you like and, if you are open, you will gain something, but don't let it end there. Reading a book like this is not just about ticking another box on your to-do list, it's about integrating the exercises and processes into your way of life.

Over the years many people have come to me with a yearning to find what is missing from their lives. If you feel the same way then you need to understand that the thing currently missing from your life is *you*. The real, authentic You. Let this book be one of the guides that allows you to find and express the real you again and help you live your life with joy, inspiration, meaning and purpose.

Mark and Andrea's Experience

Mark:

I was 42 years old and after an extended period of traumatic events and suppressed stress, my whole system shut down. Mind Body Spirit went STOP! It was clinical depression. As it cleared, I understood I couldn't continue one step further on the way I had been walking. I was a good son, a good husband, a good friend, a good employee, a good citizen… and I was dying inside. I changed things – though it terrified me. I was at the point that the fear of changing was outweighed by the fear of staying the same! I started saying 'yes' to the desire I felt inside to live my authentic life.

I flew to Thailand for three intensive weeks of yoga training, where I met and fell in love with one of the senior students, my soulmate, Andrea. We were together for my last week on the island, then I returned home to work, wishing that life could somehow bring together this Hungarian woman and this Australian man … and it did: Andrea chose to come to Australia to be with me.

After 6 months, and the death of my father, I changed the last things from my old life - quit my job, sold my car, cleared out my possessions, rented my house and we left Australia together. Once again, we headed for Thailand, more yoga and the rest of the world, with a one way ticket and no set plans.

During this time Andrea was facing her own challenges and our relationship came under enormous strain. Eventually we separated, and my world fell apart.

Andrea went to meditate and I went to India. For the first time in my life I knew I was totally alone. No parents, no siblings, no job, no partner, no comfort, no direction. I loved Andrea but there was no guarantee that this would be reciprocated. She was in silent retreat for two months and I learned more about loving unconditionally. I knew that this was my chance to find me. The Universe had given it to me, as surely as I had asked for it. It just was in a way I hadn't expected.

And so I did my practice, worked on myself, worked on making manifest all that I really was. I worked on acceptance. I grew calm, confident, positive. I was emerging.

Andrea and I re-established contact and it felt better. I flew to the Malaysian monastery to meet her. We were together again.

The same things that we sparked in each other before were still there; this time, though, there was a deeper understanding of it, and we learned to not turn it into an emotional tennis match. I started to take responsibility for myself.

I believe that the Universe wants us to be happy. That our Spirits are, at every moment, finding and giving us exactly what we need for our best evolution – regardless of what our minds think about it!

Andrea:

My own journey started at 26 when the Bulimia I had got so bad that I couldn't deny it any longer and I had to ask for help. Seeing a psychologist helped me to get in touch with my inner feelings. They very slowly developed into a trusted inner voice.

Another turning point was 3 years later when, already travelling in Asia, I did my first meditation retreat. I felt I had found something, a method, a way to find real peace and inner freedom. So I knew I had a goal … Even when I went back to Europe to earn money it was mainly just a transitory time for me to get back to my Asian retreats and yoga.

Despite my personal growth I still believed I had to walk this path alone, until I met Mark and it started to seem possible to live in a relationship. The challenges [of a relationship] came in big chunks. There was no way to hide from them anymore.

How did I overcome the challenges? With patience, perseverance, with the knowing that everything starts from within. And if I focused on myself it had to work out eventually for the two of us as well. The voice within whispered the truth. It just takes time. I started to find my true self and a clearer life path and we started breathing again. The journey of finding my personal truth was the key to everything and has helped me to feel inspired about my own life and our relationship.

So, here we are, together now, with mystery in front of us and looking to see how far this can go. Only God knows.

And it is good so far.

ANDREA K. AND MARK B.
AUSTRALASIA

Inspiring, aren't they? And even more so for being willing to share their stories so generously with us. I wish you all the best with your own journey of self discovery and living a life of inspiration.

That is my wish for you.

NAMASTÉ
BELINDAGRACE

List of Exercises

This book contains many wonderful, practical exercises to help you discover and connect to your divine inspiration.

Although the book is designed for you to work through the exercises one by one as you progress along your path, you may find in subsequent readings you wish to 'jump' to a particular exercise.

Here is the list of exercises and page numbers for easy reference.

YOU ARE CLAIRVOYANT CD

**Developing the Secret Skill
We All Have
Self Development Program
Companion CD to book**

You Are Clairvoyant CD will help you develop your own intuitive and clairvoyant skills.

We are all naturally gifted in this way, but most of us have forgotten how to use these innate human skills. With the help of this CD you can reconnect to your innate clairvoyant gifts.

To make the most of this tutorial CD it is best to listen to the instructions closely and complete only one exercise per day. It's also important to do the exercises in the order presented, so you can develop your skills from a strong foundation. Then, once you've completed each exercise at least once, you can begin to focus more on the ones that appeal to you.

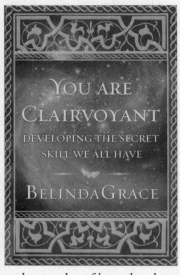

Numerology
Numbers and their influence
RoseMaree Templeton

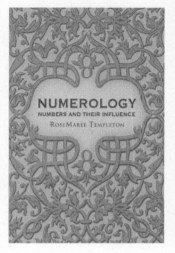

Author RoseMaree Templeton began her lifelong journey with numerology in her teens, studying under her grandmother, Hettie Templeton, Australia's foremost numerologist during the 1940s and 1950s. Rose-Maree combines Hettie's teachings with her own insights and experiences. The result is this book – a return to the basics of self-help numerology.

RoseMaree has a charm, wisdom and insight that she enjoys sharing and has guided many in making decisions about career, relationships, travel and even real estate, through her use of numerology. This book explains how the power of numerology can help people cope with everyday problems and challenges of life.

This book will show you how to:
• Calculate and interpret your ruling number, day number and destiny number
• Draw up and read birthdate and name charts
• Read pyramid charts that map peaks and troughs throughout life
• Prepare readings for yourself, family and friends

It also includes samples of charts and readings of celebrities such as musician Paul 'Bono' Hewson, former first lady of the USA Hillary Clinton, cricketer Shane Warne and Diana, Princess of Wales.

RRP $27.95
Available at all good bookstores or online at
www.rockpoolpublishing.com.au

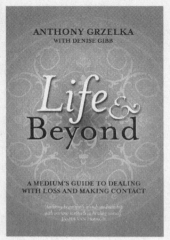

LIFE AND BEYOND
A MEDIUM'S GUIDE TO DEALING WITH LOSS AND MAKING CONTACT
Anthony Grzelka
(with Denise Gibb)

ANTHONY GRZELKA, 39-year-old father of three is one of Australia's leading spiritual Mediums. As the Australian equivalent to John Edwards, he conducts seminars, workshops and private readings throughout Australia. His private readings are booked out for two years.

His approach to helping people deal with grief and achieve spiritual wellbeing is down-to-earth, practical and achievable.

And the results, are "beyond belief" say the astonished families who've experienced Anthony's special brand of 'crossing over'. He is the man dubbed Australia's own 'Ghost Whisperer' – and the only Aussie medium endorsed by respected US medium, James Van Praagh.

LIFE AND BEYOND, A MEDIUM'S GUIDE TO DEALING WITH LOSS AND MAKING CONTACT is an interactive book that will help people to cope with grief and loss through teaching them how to make connections with the spirit world. It gives hands on grief coping initiatives and addresses many different types of loss, including grief and loss in men and how to use a medium's spirituality to recover. Accessible for all, this book will inspire people to cope with their loss by connecting to the spirit world.

RRP $24.95
Available at all good bookstores or online at
www.rockpoolpublishing.com.au
